Composting
FOR
DUMMIES®

by Cathy Cromell and the Editors of The National Gardening Association

WILEY

Wiley Publishing, Inc.

Composting For Dummies®

Published by
Wiley Publishing, Inc.
111 River St.
Hoboken, NJ 07030-5774
www.wiley.com

Copyright © 2010 by Wiley Publishing, Inc., Indianapolis, Indiana

Published simultaneously in Canada

For general information on our other products and services, please contact our Customer Care Department within the U.S. at 877-762-2974, outside the U.S. at 317-572-3993, or fax 317-572-4002.

For technical support, please visit www.wiley.com/techsupport.

Wiley also publishes its books in a variety of electronic formats. Some content that appears in print may not be available in electronic books.

Library of Congress Control Number: 2009942825

ISBN: 978-0-470-58161-2

Manufactured in the United States of America

10 9 8 7 6 5 4 3 2 1

WILEY

About the Author

Cathy Cromell is the Southwest regional reporter for the National Gardening Association (NGA). She completed the Master Composter and Master Gardener certification programs at the University of Arizona Maricopa County Cooperative Extension Urban Horticulture Department in Phoenix, where she also absorbed abundant hands-on experience hoisting tons of organic matter while overseeing the composting area of the Master Gardener Demonstration Garden.

As editor of Arizona Master Gardener Press at the Cooperative Extension, Cathy produced gardening books that received numerous awards. She was also a writer for *Better Homes and Gardens New Garden Book* and a contributing writer for *Gardening in the Southwest* (Sunset Books).

As garden editor-at-large for *Phoenix Home & Garden* magazine, Cathy enjoys helping readers — especially newcomers to the desert — uncover the mysteries of arid land growing conditions in her monthly article, *Desert Gardening 101*. She also scouts earth-friendly landscapes around the Southwest to feature in the magazine's *Garden Talks* profile. "I've never encountered a gardener who wasn't delighted to share their plant passions and gardening knowledge. Their generosity and enthusiasm inspire me to tell their stories."

The National Gardening Association (NGA) is committed to sustaining and renewing the fundamental links between people, plants, and the earth. Founded in 1972 as "Gardens for All" to spearhead the community garden movement, today's NGA promotes environmental responsibility, advances multidisciplinary learning and scientific literacy, and creates partnerships that restore and enhance communities.

NGA is best known for its garden-based curricula, educational materials, international initiatives, and several youth garden grant programs. Together, these reach more than 300,000 children nationwide each year. NGA's Web sites, one for home gardeners and another for those who garden with kids, build community and offer a wealth of custom content.

To find out more about the National Gardening Association, write to 1100 Dorset St., South Burlington, VT 05403, or visit its Web sites at www.garden.org or www.kidsgardening.org.

Dedication

To my parents, Patricia and William Cromell. Thank you for instilling me with a love of plants and nature that has sustained and nourished me throughout my life.

Author's Acknowledgments

I would like to thank Suzanne DeJohn and the National Gardening Association for this opportunity to write about one of my favorite gardening topics — the inestimable benefits of rotting organic matter.

My appreciation to the exceptionally capable folks at Wiley Publishing who helped lift this project off the ground, starting with acquisitions editor Mike Baker, who championed an entire book about composting. Project editor Elizabeth Rea performed a superlative job organizing the contents to flow logically for readers. Copy editor Christy Pingleton gave an exemplary performance polishing my rambling text. My thanks, also, to Sue Fisher for her comprehensive technical review and to Barbara Frake for her finely detailed illustrations.

I'm fortunate to know dozens of talented gardeners and horticulture professionals who generously share their knowledge and expertise with me. I offer special thanks to Carolyn Chard, Frank Martin, and Annette Weaver, who many years ago infected me with a virulent dose of their enthusiasm for composting; to Jo Cook, Mike Hills, and Kirti Mathura, who respond to my midnight e-mails with good humor and precise detail; and to Robyn Baker, Louisa Ballard, and Kathy Green, who remind me of all the truly important things in a plant addict's life.

I extend my deep appreciation to Lucy K. Bradley, PhD, who once upon a time graciously invited me to accompany her down the garden writer's path. Her creative vision and optimism continue to inspire me even though she moved to a land far, far away. I continue to be the lucky recipient of Nancy Erdman's good humor as my long-time editor at *Phoenix Home & Garden* magazine. Finally, I am especially grateful to my sister, Patricia S. Piasecki, who is a kind soul I can always rely upon. If only she lived in the same time zone, I would gladly turn her compost pile ~~every week~~ ~~month~~ ~~few months~~ once in a while.

Publisher's Acknowledgments

We're proud of this book; please send us your comments at http://dummies.custhelp.
com. For other comments, please contact our Customer Care Department within the U.S. at
877-762-2974, outside the U.S. at 317-572-3993, or fax 317-572-4002.

Some of the people who helped bring this book to market include the following:

Acquisitions, Editorial, and Media Development

Project Editor: Elizabeth Rea

Senior Acquisitions Editor: Mike Baker

Copy Editor: Christine Pingleton

Assistant Editor: Erin Calligan Mooney

Editorial Program Coordinator: Joe Niesen

Technical Editor: Sue Fisher

Editorial Manager: Michelle Hacker

Editorial Assistant: Jennette ElNaggar

Art Coordinator: Alicia B. South

Cover Photos: iStock

Cartoons: Rich Tennant
(www.the5thwave.com)

Composition Services

Project Coordinator: Sheree Montgomery

Layout and Graphics: Melissa K. Jester, Christine Williams

Special Art: Barbara Frake

Proofreader: Sossity R. Smith

Indexer: Claudia Bourbeau

Publishing and Editorial for Consumer Dummies

Diane Graves Steele, Vice President and Publisher, Consumer Dummies

Kristin Ferguson-Wagstaffe, Product Development Director, Consumer Dummies

Ensley Eikenburg, Associate Publisher, Travel

Kelly Regan, Editorial Director, Travel

Publishing for Technology Dummies

Andy Cummings, Vice President and Publisher, Dummies Technology/General User

Composition Services

Debbie Stailey, Director of Composition Services

Contents at a Glance

Table of Contents

Introduction

*E*nvironmental issues and green living have experienced an upswing in popular interest in recent years, and composting is right in the thick of it. Recycling organic wastes where they're generated, rather than transporting them to a landfill, is an integral part of today's earth-friendly lifestyle. Compost, the premium-quality end product of this process, offers a terrific bonus for your garden and landscape.

As a child growing up in Minnesota, I recall using a hand trowel to easily scoop out a transplant hole in our vegetable garden's loamy soil, but the growing season was all too brief. In Arizona, my hole-digging may start with a pickaxe, but I'm spoiled by year-round gardening. Although growing conditions differ radically from region to region or country to country, the basics of enriching garden beds with compost to produce healthy vegetables and flowers apply wherever you live. I hope this book helps you become a composting convert and more successful gardener.

About This Book

This book is for people who, like Rumpelstiltskin of fairy tale fame, want to turn straw into gold. Well, black gold anyway, which is what savvy gardeners call their compost. This book gives you the keys to transform what some see as useless organic refuse — yard trimmings, grass clippings, kitchen scraps, and of course, straw — into a valuable stash of black, crumbly compost for improving your soil and nourishing your plants.

If you picked up this book out of curiosity and composting is new to you, don't feel intimidated. There's nothing difficult or mysterious about it: Everything organic decomposes eventually. This book guides you every step of the way to help your composting process be productive and trouble-free.

Conventions Used in This Book

You can compost organic matter in all sorts of receptacles. I use the terms *bin, container,* and *unit* interchangeably to signify something that corrals your compost materials more neatly than a free-standing heap.

When I mention *county cooperative extension office,* I'm referring to university-sponsored outreach programs in the United States that are free to the public in all 50 states. Many offices also train Master Gardener volunteers to answer questions about composting as well as other horticultural topics. Canadian Master Gardener volunteers are affiliated with varied organizations, including universities and public gardens. Use your favorite Internet search engine to locate these programs in your region.

You'll find the following other conventions used throughout this book to call attention to specific information:

- ✔ New terms being defined are highlighted in *italics.*
- ✔ **Boldfaced** text indicates the action part of numbered steps or key text in bulleted lists.
- ✔ Monofont is used for Web addresses.

What You're Not to Read

Feel free to skip anything marked with a Technical Stuff icon or appearing in a shaded sidebar. I think this information is interesting, but you don't have to know it to be a successful composter.

Foolish Assumptions

I think it's a tad rude to make assumptions about you when we've never met, but my publisher insists! So, here's what I assumed about you in writing this book:

- ✔ You want to save money by producing your own nutrient-rich compost to use as a soil amendment or to enhance soil fertility.
- ✔ You want to generate lots of lovely compost to grow the best flower, vegetable, or herb beds in the neighborhood.
- ✔ You're concerned about the environment and want to do your part to reduce the amount of organic waste sent to landfills.
- ✔ You follow the philosophy of "Reduce, Reuse, Recycle" in other areas of your life and want to add composting to the list.
- ✔ You want a family-friendly activity that helps your children (or grandchildren) understand nature's own recycling process.
- ✔ You don't live where local government offers collection of kitchen scraps or food waste for community composting.
- ✔ You want to get more exercise and fresh air, while still doing something productive!

How This Book Is Organized

This book is separated into five major parts, each one covering a general topic related to composting. Take a look at the part summaries that follow, and head to whatever part sounds like it best addresses your composting needs.

Part 1: Composting Basics

If you're curious as to why composting matters, this part starts with an explanation of the problems caused by sending yard trimmings and kitchen waste to landfills. It describes how you can help alleviate those problems by composting organic waste at home. In this part I also cover the basic tools needed to compost. Rotting organic matter provides a livelihood for billions of decomposer organisms, and they receive their 15 minutes of fame in this part as well.

Part II: Selecting a Home and Method for Your Compost

Here's where you get help to decide where to compost: aboveground, in a hole, or within the confines of a container. Or perhaps you'll take up kitchen composting, which also uses containers. In addition to a rundown of your manufactured container options, this part also includes a chapter on the variety of containers you can construct yourself.

Part III: Compost Happens

Flip to this section to find out what ingredients can go into your compost pile, what stays out, and how to mix it all up in the right proportions based upon your schedule. You also get recommendations on what to do with all that compost you're churning out.

Part IV: Expanding Your Compost Horizons

These chapters describe other methods to process kitchen waste or add organic matter to the soil. I explain vermicomposting — working with composting worms that eat your garbage. If you want to add more organic matter to your soil than your traditional compost pile can generate, take a look at the chapters in this part explaining cover crops or green manures, and sheet composting or composting mulch.

Part V: The Part of Tens

Head straight to the troubleshooting tips if your compost pile isn't cooperating with you. You'll also find the answers to ten quick FAQs for an overview of composting basics.

Icons Used in This Book

This book contains icons that flag noteworthy bits of information. This is the type of information you can expect from these icons:

 This is where I include easy-to-follow suggestions to save you time, effort, or money. They include a few gems from my own experience that I wish someone had shared with me years ago!

 This is the need-to-know, key information to retain about composting.

 This icon serves as an alert to avoid potentially unpleasant or unsafe activities. It also steers you clear of practices that impede your efforts to produce compost in a timely fashion.

 Sometimes it's helpful or fun to understand a little more than "how-to" information and delve into the "whys" behind a particular process. This icon highlights information that you don't need to know but may find useful.

Where to Go from Here

I hope you're excited to dive into composting. And I hope you aren't afraid of doing something wrong. Decomposition of organic matter is a natural process that's going to happen regardless of what you do. But you can help it along, so this book guides you along the most direct path to problem-free composting. It's designed so that you can absorb info from any chapter that catches your eye.

If you want to understand how decomposition really happens and are interested in microscopic organisms, head straight to Chapter 3. If you want to start composting with the least amount of effort, check out Chapter 4, which describes a freestanding heap. If you're curious about containers, jump to Chapters 5 and 6. If you're looking for a fun activity with kids (that might teach them a little something when they aren't suspecting it), check out Chapter 10 on composting with worms. Otherwise, thumb through the book until something catches your fancy.

Part I
Composting Basics

In this part...

This part is designed for people who like to "begin at the beginning." It leads off with a discussion of the wide-ranging benefits of composting, to you and your garden, your local community, and yes, even the planet. I don't bombard you with statistics, but I hope this information inspires you to become a compost convert.

I also include lists of a few items that keep you safe and sound while composting, as well as the minimal tools required for maintaining your pile. I introduce you to the fascinating — and crowded — world of the soil food web that is alive and thriving in your compost pile. You discover a varied cast of characters, such as sweet-smelling bacteria and scared roly-polies. You may work up a healthy sweat turning your compost pile, but it's the billions of minuscule creatures living within it that are doing the real heavy lifting.

Chapter 1

Digging into Compost

*Y*ou can't fail at composting. Isn't that a nice thing to know at the start of a project? Organic matter will rot no matter what you do. Fuss over it daily or ignore it for months; it doesn't matter. So, dig right in and enjoy the process!

This chapter defines a few terms, briefly introduces the soil food web, and gives you a quick description of hot and cold composting methods. The remainder of the chapter covers some of the many benefits of compost and composting.

Welcome to the World of Compost

Decomposition of organic matter is an essential biological process that's ongoing in every nook and cranny of the planet. *Composting* is a method for you to copy nature's process, speeding it up if you so choose, to ultimately reap a rich mound of soil-enhancing compost for your landscape.

What compost is

A beneficial, soil-like substance, *compost* is a mixture of decayed and decaying organic matter that improves soil structure and provides nutrients for plants.

If compost is the end product of your composting effort, what, then, is humus? Compost and humus are terms that are often used interchangeably, although there are subtle differences. Have you ever taken a stroll in the woods and uncovered fallen leaves to spy a rich layer of crumbly, sweet-smelling, black earth? That's *humus,* which is comprised of well-decomposed plant and animal matter. Resembling dark coffee grounds, humus is aromatic, lightweight, and spongy in texture, allowing it to hold water.

Compost resembles humus but is comprised of materials in various stages of decomposition. Some may be broken down quickly; others may require multiple rounds of destruction from varied specialized microorganisms and soil invertebrates. A pile of compost may contain some humus, but there's still plenty of work available in the heap for the decomposers.

Don't let the fact that not all the contents of your compost are fully decomposed stop you from incorporating compost into your garden. In fact, it's a good thing to do because your compost's abundant microbial activity provides benefits to your soil, which I cover later in the chapter.

What tools and equipment you need

You don't need to buy a lot of stuff to begin composting. In fact, you could get started with nothing more than that old shovel propped in the corner of your shed or garage. However, it's much easier — and more entertaining — with a few well-chosen implements, such as a pitchfork and compost thermometer. I describe the most useful tools to enhance your composting experience later in Part I. The list is short, so no need to worry if your wallet is thin!

You may also have questions about compost bins. Are they essential? No, but depending on style, containers use space efficiently, provide a tidy appearance, and help you maintain moisture and heat within your heap of organic matter, ultimately producing compost faster. Some container styles also do a good job of deterring pests, if that's a concern where you live. In Part II, I cover characteristics of all sorts of home-built and manufactured bins and offer guidance for selecting the ideal container for your needs.

How composting works

Composting works best when you mix up the right combinations of organic matter and living conditions for the soil microorganisms and invertebrates performing all the decomposing work.

It may be easy to forget that soil is brimming with life when most of its occupants are microscopic. Imagine the most crowded city street or subway you've ever tried to negotiate at rush hour. That's a stroll in an empty wilderness compared to the multitudes of soil dwellers living beneath your feet. A single gram of soil — about the size of a navy bean — holds 100 million to 1 billion bacteria, 100,000 to 1 million fungi, 1,000 to 1 million algae, and 1,000 to 100,000 protozoa.

The soil's microscopic multitudes share space with larger invertebrates, many of whom you can see with the naked eye, such as springtails, mites, and beetles. Populations of microscopic organisms and soil invertebrates create a diverse and highly functioning soil food web (see Chapter 3 for more details). And they're the same fascinating creatures that convert your yard wastes and kitchen scraps to useful compost.

You Can Do It! Home Composting Made Easy

I delve into more detail about hot and cold composting methods in this section, but if you're eager to get started, jump ahead to Chapter 4 to find basic instructions for creating a simple, free-standing pile.

Some like it hot!

As microorganisms begin breaking down organic matter, they release heat as a byproduct of their activity. If you build a pile with the right mix of ingredients, moisture, and air, it quickly reaches 120 degrees Fahrenheit (49 degrees Celsius) and higher and may heat up sufficiently to kill weed seeds or pathogens. This is known as *hot* or *thermophilic composting.* Specialized microorganisms known as *thermophiles* (heat-lovers) survive those high temps and continue eating and reproducing until the conditions are no longer favorable — that is, when your pile runs out of food, water, and air.

You can manage your composting to maintain relatively high temperatures by mixing and remoistening (as needed) until the preferred food sources are depleted. At that point, temperatures start dropping, and different microorganisms known as *mesophiles* (which thrive in moderate temperatures) take over. Soil invertebrates also arrive when temperatures drop to join in the decomposition process. Hot composting produces useable compost in as little as 3 or 4 weeks up to 2 or 3 months.

Cool customers

In cold or slow composting systems, it may take 6 to 12 months or even longer to obtain useable compost. Piles don't heat up sufficiently to kill weed seeds or pathogens. However, the advantage is that the pile requires no maintenance on your part after you build it. Even though you aren't turning the pile to improve aeration or adding moisture, decomposer organisms will continue to break down the refuse. Mesophile and *psychrophiles* (cold-loving organisms) perform the work at a slower pace.

Vermicomposting (worm composting) and most forms of *sheet composting* (spreading organic material on top of the soil to decompose in place) are considered cold systems. Because they vary from the traditional approach of working with a pile, these methods are covered in their own chapters.

Reaping the Rewards of Composting

Composting saves you money, reduces global warming, helps you lose weight, and improves your love life! All right, there might be some exaggeration in that statement, but given a choice between composting and product infomercials blaring similar claims, I'd go with composting because it

- ✔ Saves money by cutting trash collection fees and reducing, or eliminating, the need to buy soil amendments, conditioners, and fertilizers. You can also save on your water bill because incorporating compost into your soil improves its moisture-holding capacity.

- ✔ Reduces the amount of methane (a greenhouse gas) produced when organic matter decomposes in landfills.

- ✔ Burns about 350 calories per hour as you turn the pile (for a person weighing 150 pounds).

- ✔ Might get you noticed by someone who cares about one of the previous three items.

Still not convinced? This section offers more good reasons to take up composting.

A healthier, more prolific garden

If you want to grow a fabulous vegetable, flower, or herb garden, start with your soil. Healthy, fertile soil equals healthy, productive plants. And the best thing you can do to create healthy garden soil is to add compost. Here's what compost will do for your beds:

✔ **Add organic matter to improve soil structure and porosity:**
Soil is made up of sand, silt, and clay particles. Soil structure
refers to the arrangement of these particles — how they
aggregate or clump together and form pore spaces that permit
air and water flow through the soil. Soil porosity creates a
healthy environment for plant roots to thrive. Incorporating
compost helps sandy soil retain moisture and nutrients so
you may be able to water and fertilize less frequently. Adding
compost also loosens compacted clay soil, reduces erosion,
and promotes better drainage so plant roots don't rot in
overly wet soil.

✔ **Add and feed beneficial soil microorganisms:** Compost is
chock-full of beneficial microbes that add life to your garden
soil. When you add compost to your soil, the microbes continue breaking down organic matter to release nutrients and
even keep "bad" organisms in check.

✔ **Provide slow-release nutrients:** Because its nutrient content
varies widely based on the original ingredients and decomposition process, compost is considered a soil amendment,
not a fertilizer. Even so, compost contains essential plant
nutrients and trace elements to improve soil fertility. Also,
compost releases its nutrients slowly while it decomposes further in your soil. Garden plants make use of the nutrients over
a longer growing season. Most chemical fertilizers release
their nutrients in a quick burst; some of the value may be lost
if plants aren't ready to utilize it or heavy rains or excessive
irrigation leach it away.

A healthier community and planet

The many virtues of composting reach beyond improving individual gardens. Composting your yard waste and kitchen scraps at
home, rather than setting them out for trash collection, offers you
an avenue to be a part of the solution for issues such as overbur-
dened landfills, pollution, and global warming. Here are a few reasons to divert your compostable organic materials from heading to
the landfill:

✔ Composting extends the life of existing landfills and reduces
the need to create others.

✔ Composting reduces transportation costs and related air pol-
lutants from trash collection and hauling.

✔ As organic waste decomposes in landfills, it generates acidic
liquid *(leachate)* that may combine with other contaminants
in the landfill and seep into groundwater supplies.

✔ Organic waste that is tightly compressed in landfills to decompose without oxygen produces methane, which is a greenhouse gas.

✔ Burning yard waste is not a suitable option for disposal in urban areas, because it pollutes the air and exacerbates problems for people with allergies, bronchitis, asthma, and other respiratory issues. Burning waste is also banned in some rural areas, so composting is a good alternative.

✔ A compost heap is a wonderful wildlife habitat that teems with invertebrates and makes a snug home for beneficial creatures such as toads that provide free insect control in your garden.

Yard waste includes any type of organic residue from landscaping or gardening activities: pruned branches, spent plants, dead flowers, grass clippings, twigs, leaves, and weeds. Many of our commonly accepted landscaping practices generate enormous piles of organic waste. For example, freshly mown grass clippings or autumn leaves are raked, stuffed into plastic bags, and piled high at curbside for trash pickup. According to the U.S. Environmental Protection Agency, 12.8 percent of municipal solid waste generated in 2007 consisted of yard waste!

I won't bury you beneath a mountain of statistics, but there's good news to report. Yard waste is biodegradable and clean (as in nonhazardous), making it perfectly suited for composting rather than transporting it to landfills. More people seem to be accepting that idea. In 2000, 56.9 percent of yard trimmings were "recovered" as compost in municipal programs. That's a giant leap in ten years from 1990's recovery rate of a paltry 12 percent.

Composting organic waste is also on the rise in Canada and the United Kingdom. In 2000, the average Canadian sent 32 kilograms of organic materials to centralized composting facilities. In 2004, the amount jumped to 51 kilograms. In the 10-year period from 1997 through 2006, recycled green waste collected in England jumped from 347,455 metric tons to 2,212,600 metric tons.

Whether you compost at home or have access to community collection programs, transforming your organic waste into beneficial compost is an earth-friendly path to take on behalf of future generations.

Soil characteristics of the American West and Southwest

If soil native to arid climates was a paint color, it could be marketed as "Boring Beige" or "Drab Dirt." Most gardeners in the arid West and Southwest regions of the United States encounter significantly different soil characteristics than gardening compatriots in other areas. Folks who relocate from regions where easily plunging a spade into dark soil is the expected norm are often flabbergasted when they have to wield a pickaxe to chip a dent in hard, rocky, organic-matter-challenged soil at their new abode. However, that doesn't mean it isn't good soil. It just has different characteristics.

That black earth in other regions forms because native plants drop large amounts of litter. All that organic matter continuously decomposes with the aid of plentiful precipitation, and over eons it builds layers of rich topsoil. In comparison, the desert's native plants drop insignificant organic matter. Consider the teensy leaf size of a mesquite tree versus a maple tree's large leaf, or the barely noticeable plant litter at the base of a cactus versus the thick bed of needles surrounding a pine tree. Also, extreme aridity slows the rate of decomposition. Mother Nature just doesn't have sufficient organic matter and moisture to work with! Consequently, arid-land soils may contain less than one-half of 1 percent organic matter.

Lack of organic matter contributes to a lack of nitrogen in desert soils. Although nitrogen is one of the primary elements required for plant growth, native trees and shrubs seldom suffer from nitrogen deficiency. They've either evolved to thrive without much nitrogen, as cacti do, or they make their own. Many arid-land plants are legumes, such as acacia and mesquite, which manufacture nitrogen in their root systems with the aid of soil bacteria.

Another common characteristic of arid-land soil is alkalinity, ranging from 8 to 8.5 on the pH scale. (pH is a measure of acidity or alkalinity. On the scale of 0–14, 7 is neutral, below 7 is acidic, and above 7 is alkaline.) Soil's pH level affects a plant's ability to absorb nutrients.

Native and desert-adapted plants readily absorb what they need from existing soils. The challenge occurs if you try to grow plants native to different climates and soils, which includes many favorite annual vegetables and flowers. Annuals, by definition, complete their life cycle in one relatively-short growing season. To fuel this furious growth spurt, you must enrich your arid-land garden beds with compost.

Composting with kids

The National Gardening Association (NGA) offers a wealth of resources to parents and educators to help them engage children in gardening activities, including composting and vermicomposting. At NGA's Kids Gardening Web site (www. kidsgardening.org), you can find project ideas, suggestions to tie composting activities to curriculum requirements, grant sources for financial and material assistance, and real-life experiences.

One inspirational story comes from a Simi Valley, California, teacher. Over a period of several years, her sixth-grade classes progressed from observing a handful of red wiggler worms process food scraps in plastic soda bottles to designing a vermicomposting system that could handle their cafeteria waste to ultimately starting a worm-based business. Vermicomposting activities in the classroom gave students a hands-on laboratory of scientific exploration that offered opportunities to teach skills in all basic subjects.

But garden-based learning offers benefits beyond the 3 Rs. In a survey conducted by NGA, garden program leaders reported remarkable improvement in essential life skills that are not easily taught to youngsters. They noted participant improvements in the following characteristics: environmental attitudes, 96 percent; community spirit, 92 percent; self-confidence, 89 percent; social skills, 87 percent; leadership skills, 85 percent; attitude towards school, 82 percent; volunteerism, 81 percent; nutritional attitudes, 77 percent; motor skills, 65 percent; and scholastic achievement, 63 percent.

You don't have to be an experienced teacher to share the world of composting and gardening with a new generation. Often it's the simple things that spark enthusiasm and set kids off on a path of natural discovery. For example, a friend of mine took her compost crank (see Chapter 2) when giving an outdoor demonstration to kids. They were thrilled with the opportunity to stir the compost, and she reported they didn't want to give it up when she was ready to leave!

Chapter 2

Tools of the Trade

. . . .

In This Chapter

▶ Safeguarding your well-being while composting

▶ Choosing useful, good-quality tools

▶ Keeping your tools in top-notch shape

. . . .

*I*f you're already gardening, chances are you can dive right into composting with tools you have on hand. But if you're new to both gardening and composting, you'll be happy to hear that you don't need to break your bank to create a tool arsenal.

This chapter shows that the supervision of rotting organic matter requires only a few basic tools! Many tools have names that are used interchangeably or differ regionally, so I help you sort that out. You also get recommendations on features to look for when purchasing quality tools, as well as steps to take to keep them in good condition. And because safety should always be your number one concern, the chapter starts off with a few basics on staying safe and healthy in the garden.

Protecting Yourself from the Elements: Safety Gear

Composting is fun! You can keep it that way with a few simple precautions: Wear gloves and other safety gear as needed, and protect yourself from the sun.

Getting a good pair of gloves

Some women have lots of shoes in the closet. I have lots of garden gloves on the shelf. I seldom pass a display of gardening gloves without stopping to try them on. Good-fitting, comfortable gloves are essential for your gardening and composting work. If they don't "feel right" in the midst of your task, you're likely to pull them off, toss them aside (forgetting where you left them), and have no protection from scratches, scrapes, and blisters. Sure, you can pick up an inexpensive pair of cotton gloves at the hardware store or nursery to get started, but upgrading to better-quality gloves when you find a pair that suits you is worthwhile. Manufacturers have been combining useful design features with diverse materials to create a whole new batch of glove styles that protect hands while still providing much-needed comfort and flexibility. Here's a rundown of your options and my recommendations:

✔ **Glove materials**

- Goatskin containing natural lanolin creates soft, supple leather that fits like, well, like a glove.

- Leather treated during the tanning process to be water-repellent and hand-washable ensures that the gloves don't turn into adobe brick as some leather gloves do if they get wet in the garden. Leather gloves also offer some protection against thorns.

- Four-way stretch nylon (the same fabric used for a lot of athletic gear) fits smoothly across the back of the hand.

✔ **Glove features**

- Padded palms offer comfort and gripping power when performing repetitive turning and digging chores.

- Longer wrists with a stretchy loop-and-tape closure lock out dirt and make taking the gloves off and pulling them back on quick and easy.

- Longer length gloves (sometimes referred to as *gauntlets*) cover all or part of the forearm (most gloves finish at the wrist). This type is especially useful when dealing with lots of thorny prunings.

- Reinforced fingertips add protection and longevity.

- Waterproof liners keep water out and warmth in.

Shielding your eyes

If you chop compost ingredients — either with a hand tool or chipper/shredder machine — always wear safety glasses or goggles to protect your eyes from errant UFOs (unidentified flying organics). Make sure you also wear these glasses when dealing with piles of long, thin, or thorny stems that could easily whip back and hit you in the eye. Safety glasses also come in handy when you turn dry organic matter that churns a lot of dust particles into the air. If allergies are a problem, safety glasses (along with a dust mask) may help prevent red, runny eyes or other symptoms. You can pick up an inexpensive pair of safety glasses at a hardware or home improvement store.

Donning a dust mask

Depending on the ingredients in your compost pile and where you garden, turning organic matter may stir up dust particles, pollen, or mold spores that can be easily inhaled. Shredding leaves and chopping organic matter also creates fine bits of drifting material. If you have allergies, asthma, or other respiratory issues, don a dust mask to protect yourself during these composting activities. You can purchase inexpensive paper dust masks from hardware and paint stores or search online for many higher-quality options.

If you have allergies or respiratory issues, the following ideas may help you enjoy your gardening activities with fewer airborne problems:

- ✔ Sprinkle the compost pile with water as you work, to hold down dust and debris.

- ✔ Refrain from turning piles on windy days.

- ✔ Work outdoors after rain showers, because rain and humidity dampen the flight of windborne pollen.

- ✔ Limit gardening activities in the early morning (5 to 10 a.m.), when most pollen is released.

- ✔ Shower and change your clothes immediately after working in the garden.

Blocking harmful rays with a hat and sunscreen

If you're a northern-climate gardener, you may be scratching your head (or rolling your eyes) about my next suggestion. But the sun's ultraviolet rays are damaging no matter where you live, and skin cancer rates are up around the globe. Protect yourself by

- ✔ Wearing a wide-brimmed hat

- ✔ Slathering on sunscreen with an SPF of at least 15

- ✔ Staying out of the sun from 10 a.m. to 2 p.m., when the rays are most damaging

- ✔ Wearing long-sleeved shirts and long pants

Even if you think you're just going out to the compost pile "for a minute," it's easy to become engrossed (compost is fascinating stuff), and two hours can sweep by before you know it. Please protect yourself, and stay hydrated with lots of drinking water!

Choosing the Right Tools and Equipment for the Job

All you really need to get composting is a long-handled fork, a spade or shovel, and something with which to chop up larger stems and prunings. But like most jobs in the garden, having the right tools for the task makes it a whole lot easier. This section guides you to select tools that are best for your composting efforts. Tool descriptions may also mention other common gardening tasks that they're designed for because if you're shopping for tools, this information may help you decide which styles offer the most bang for your buck.

Mixing things up with a pitchfork or compost fork

You only need one fork to get started composting, and because the features of various forks are so similar, I describe them together. Pitchforks and compost forks have four or five long, thin, tapered, and upward-curving tines designed to efficiently glide into a pile of organic material, allowing you to hoist and pitch it to a new location. These forks are perfect for moving large clumps of bulky, lightweight organic matter, such as hay, straw, leaves, and plant trimmings. Use them to build new compost piles and turn them until the organic matter is fairly decomposed. Then it's time to switch to a shovel or soil fork for turning almost-finished compost one last time, or moving finished compost into the garden.

The primary differences between a pitchfork and a compost fork are the handle length and shape. Pitchfork handles are usually about 4 feet (1.2 meters) long with a straight end. Compost fork handles are usually shorter — about 3 feet (1 meter) long — with a D-grip end. Also, pitchforks generally have narrower tool heads than compost forks.

Digging in with a soil fork

Also known as a *digging fork* or *spading fork,* this tool's flattened prongs are shorter, thicker, and sturdier than pitchfork or compost fork tines. A soil fork is useful for turning almost-finished compost or digging heavy finished compost from the pile and incorporating it into garden beds. Soil forks also are terrific tools for plunging into compacted soil to loosen it when creating a new planting area. They can be used to break up clods and clumps of soil and dig up weedy patches, making it easy to pull handfuls of weeds and shake the soil off their roots. The shorter tines of soil forks don't work as well as pitchforks and compost forks for moving loads of unde-composed organic matter, but they do a decent job of scooping up small piles of annuals or weeds pulled from the garden.

Getting the lowdown on shovels and spades

The words "shovel" and "spade" are sometimes used interchange-ably, and the terminology may vary by region as well. Generally, though, a shovel is a tool designed for moving material, with a raised lip on each side of the blade to stop bits from falling off. A spade has a sharp, straight head and is used for digging. As previ-ously described with forks, a spade can be used for shifting mate-rial both before and after composting, although not so efficiently.

Both shovels and spades are available in various styles, with slight variations to enhance specific gardening tasks, such as trenching for irrigation lines, edging lawns, or transplanting perennials. Table 2-1 notes a few characteristics to help you sort them out.

Table 2-1   Characteristics of Shovels versus Spades

Shovels	*Spades*
Have long handles — about 48 inches (1.2 meters)	Have shorter handles — about 28 inches (70 centimeters)
Have straight handles	Have D-grip handles
Have an angled neck for scooping and tossing soil	Have a straight neck for digging into soil

Rounded-blade shovel

A rounded-blade shovel serves as an all-purpose tool for gardening tasks such as turning almost-finished compost, shoveling finished compost from a bin, incorporating compost into garden beds, and digging transplant holes in already-loose, sandy, or loamy soils.

Pointed-blade shovel

A pointed-blade shovel is the most versatile choice if you buy only one digging implement. It performs the same chores as the rounded-blade shovel, while also allowing easier digging into compacted clay soils. The pointed blade is useful for chopping up organic matter into smaller pieces before tossing it into the compost pile, although the square-blade spade, which I describe next, does a better job with this task. A pointed-blade shovel is also helpful for slicing through root balls when dividing perennials.

Square-blade digging spade

Typically used for loosening and digging soil in garden beds, the square-blade spade's shorter handle length and flat blade edge also facilitate chopping up organic matter into bits and pieces for speedier decomposition. (See other chopping options later in this chapter.) The handle grips on these short, square-blade spades are either smooth and straight, as they are on the rounded- and pointed-blade shovels, or they have a D-grip, which gives you extra gripping power as you wield the tool as a chopper.

Buy a spade with a *boot tread,* which is a thicker top edge that allows your foot to push against the blade with more power. This characteristic is especially helpful if you garden where soils are hard, rocky, or compacted.

Investing in a good-quality hose

In composting, easy access to water is important because moisture is an essential component of a successful composting effort, and it's likely that you'll need to moisten the organic matter periodically to keep it decomposing properly. A cheap hose will plague you forever, kinking, cracking, and refusing to coil easily until you finally give up and buy a better one. Splurge on a good-quality hose at the outset and add a nozzle that allows you to turn the flow on and off to conserve water while you work, as well as adjust the settings for different watering chores in the garden. For composting, a fine spray works great to gently moisten everything without wasting water as you work. Nozzles are available in a wide range of styles and prices.

You can buy hoses with or without reels, but for your main hose a reel is strongly recommended. It enables you to coil and store your hose quickly, easily, and neatly, and it also extends the life of the hose. Choose from free-standing or wall-mounted reels; some retract automatically while others have to be wound manually.

You can extend the life of your hose by following these simple guidelines:

✔ Don't leave a hose lying in direct sun.

✔ Drain a hose before winter weather sets in, and store it indoors during the off-season.

✔ Don't drag a hose over rocky surfaces.

✔ Coil a hose when not in use.

Water pressure decreases as the hose gets longer, so purchase a hose that is only as long as you need.

Moving compost in buckets or tarps

Compost transport around the garden can be as thrifty and low-tech as a heavy-duty plastic builder's bucket (not a lightweight household one) or a tarp. A bucket is ideal for moving small quantities of compost. As for bigger loads, of course it will take time and labor to transfer lots of compost with just a bucket or two, but think of all the wonderful free exercise you'll get.

Check out a garden supply store for sturdy tarps or carry bags with reinforced corner handles that allow you to gather up the corners and drag the bundle by yourself or carry it between two people. Another option is a contractor-grade polyethylene tarp with reinforced grommets in the corners. They may come with their own handles or you can slip nylon rope or lengths of cloth through the grommets to make your own. Polyethylene tarps are waterproof and tear-resistant.

Tarps are also great for tossing over compost piles to maintain moisture in arid climates and prevent excess moisture from turning your compost into a soggy mess in rainy climates. Also, covering a newly constructed pile with a tarp helps retain heat as the decomposition process gets underway. Polyethylene works best as a cover, but burlap is better than nothing!

Hauling compost with wheelbarrows or garden carts

If you generate a lot of compost and have a big yard with lots of plants and planting areas to haul your lovely compost to, a wheelbarrow or garden cart is an asset. They come in all sorts of variations, sizes, and weights.

Most wheelbarrows have one tire, positioned in front, and you lift the back end up off the ground to push it along. (Although two-wheeler wheelbarrows are also available, they're typically construction-grade to support heavy loads. You still have to lift and push.) Wheelbarrows are less stable than garden carts, but more maneuverable in tight spaces. Depending on their weight and that of the materials within, dumping everything out by tipping the wheelbarrow up on end is fairly easy.

When you've seen one wheelbarrow, you've pretty much seen them all, but garden carts offer a diverse range of styles. Carts distribute the weight of the load over two and sometimes four wheels, making them steadier to control than wheelbarrows. Carts can be pushed or pulled, and some can be towed by lawn tractors or even bicycles if you're so inclined. Their typically rectangular or boxy shape doesn't allow quite the same maneuverability for backing up and spinning around in tight quarters as wheelbarrows do. Some garden carts look like crossbreeds with wheelbarrows, but have deeper beds and wider wheel platforms for stability. Some carts can be lifted and dumped like wheelbarrows; others have panels that flip up or can be removed completely for ease in loading and unloading. Other styles fold up for storage during the off-season.

The following questions can help you sort out the best choice for your needs when purchasing either a wheelbarrow or garden cart:

- How much weight and volume does it hold?
- How much weight can you comfortably push or pull?
- Will its dimensions travel easily through areas in your yard, such as between garden rows or into the tight corner where the compost bins are?
- How sturdy are the wheels? Will they support a heavy load without collapsing? Look for wide tires with tread if you need traction on slopes.
- What is the construction material? Will it hold up in your climate?
- Are the handles comfortable to grip?
- Are metal parts rust-resistant?

Additional Gadgets and Tools for the Enthusiastic Composter

Compost will make itself without the aid of any gadgets, but if you want to speed things up a bit or just get up close and personal with your heap, check out the additional tools and gadgets covered in this section.

Testing your compost's temperature

I'm not much for gadgets, but I do love my compost thermometer. Mounted on the end of a long probe (about 20 inches, or 0.5 meter), this thermometer is ideal for sticking into the center of a pile to monitor its temperature. (Read all about it in Chapter 8.)

Aerating your compost

The best method for incorporating more air into your compost is to turn the pile completely, as I describe in Chapter 8. But if you don't have the time or inclination to turn it, an aerating tool may be useful. An *aerating crank,* also known as a *compost crank,* works on the principle that it's easier to plunge a long implement deep within the organic matter to poke around — especially within the confines of a small and narrow bin — than it is to stir things up from above with a pitchfork or shovel. Cranks operate like giant corkscrews (see Figure 2-1). You stick the tool on top of the compost, turn the handle to drill it through the organic matter, and then pull it out or unscrew it by turning the handle in the reverse direction.

While shopping for composting equipment, you may encounter an aerating tool somewhat resembling a harpoon. Paddles lie flush with the tool as you plunge it through the organic matter. As you pull the tool back out, the paddles pop out to the sides to catch and move organic matter. The harpoon aerators I've tried require more physical effort than a compost crank, and the paddles have repeatedly gotten stuck in chunky or woody material, making the tool troublesome to pull out. If you're a big burly weightlifter, yanking out a stuck aerating tool may be of no consequence! But if you're puny (like me) or have back or shoulder problems, the harpoon style may not suit you.

Bear in mind that, depending on where you live, your heap is very likely to become home to all sorts of creatures, from frogs and toads to hedgehogs, particularly in winter. Stirring up your heap could disturb or even kill them.

Considering chopping tools

You don't need chopping tools to be an effective composter. As I describe earlier in the chapter, pointed- and square-blade shovels can chop weeds and plant material. As you trim plants, you can use pruners and loppers for reducing organic matter into smaller pieces. However, if you have lots of organic matter to dice and slice, other tool options include a machete or a cutter mattock (see Figure 2-1).

Machetes and cutter mattocks are sharp tools that can cause serious injury, so caution is required.

✒ **Machete:** You've likely seen an actor in a movie whacking through dense jungle foliage with a machete. This long-bladed knife works fine for chopping up garden refuse. Sizes vary, but a machete blade is usually about 15 to 20 inches (38 to 51 centimeters), plus a 5- to 6-inch (12- to 15-centimeter) handle. You need a flat, stable chopping surface to lay the material on for chopping. I know a gardener who chops on an old tree stump. Rather than paying someone to grind the stump out, she'll have chipped away most of it herself in a few years.

✒ **Cutter mattock:** A cutter mattock has a cutting edge blade similar to a small axe, which works well for chopping organic matter. Its second blade is usually an adz blade, used for digging in hard soil or hoeing. Mattock tool heads weigh from 3 to 7 pounds (1.5 to 3 kilograms) and handles are about 3 to 4 feet (1 to 1.2 meters) long.

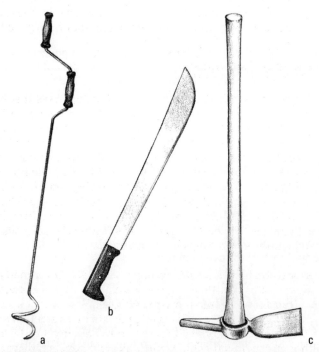

Figure 2-1: Helpful tools for composters: compost crank (a), machete (b), and cutter mattock (c).

Tool-Buying Tips

A specialized tool seems to be available for just about every garden task. If your current urge is to simplify rather than line the garage wall with more gadgets, carefully consider what types of gardening tasks you perform on a regular basis. Then purchase good-quality tools to help those chores go smoothly. The following sections address questions to ask yourself when evaluating a particular tool.

How does it feel?

A tool works best when it's comfortable for you to use, and only you can make that determination. Head to the store, remove the tool from its hook or bin, and heft it. Do the weight and balance feel right? Is the length appropriate? Because many gardening chores are repetitive, using tools that are too heavy or awkward in any way causes muscle strain, so if a tool doesn't feel right, don't buy it. There's amazing diversity in the tool market these days, so take the time to select a good-quality tool that feels good to you.

How's it made?

For strength and long-lasting durability, select tools that have the *blade* (the tool head) and the *collar* (the means by which the blade attaches to the handle) forged in one piece of metal. *Forged* tools are heavier and stronger than tools that are *stamped* (basically cut and bent) from a sheet of metal. Although less expensive, stamped tools are weaker and less durable. Examine how the tool head is attached to the handle. Better-quality tools have handles with either solid-strap or solid-socket attachments, as shown in Figure 2-2. A solid-strap handle has a metal tongue extending from the blade into the handle and secured with a rivet. A solid-socket handle inserts into a closed metal tube.

High-carbon forged steel is strong and allows you to maintain a sharp blade over time. Stainless steel tools are also good and offer the added benefit of rust resistance. However, it's somewhat more difficult to keep a sharp edge on stainless steel than on carbon. Aluminum typically is not sturdy enough for the long haul, although recent innovations such as aluminum and magnesium alloy offer durability with less overall weight.

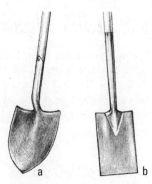

Figure 2-2: Solid-strap (a) and solid-socket (b) handles.

Materials-wise, most handle choices are either hardwood or fiberglass. Ash and hickory are the strongest hardwoods for tool handles. However, fiberglass handles are stronger and last longer. If you're lax about maintaining tools or returning them to the tool shed at the end of the day, fiberglass may be a better investment in the long run. Compare the differences:

✔ **Hardwood tool handles**

- Are less expensive than fiberglass

- Absorb the shock of repetitive motions (such as dig, lift, toss, dig, lift, toss) to reduce muscle fatigue

- Require seasonal maintenance to prevent cracking

- Can be cut to size for a more comfortable fit

✔ **Fiberglass tool handles**

- Are more expensive than hardwood

- Are lightweight, but don't absorb the shock of repetitive movements

- Are maintenance-free

- Sport bright-colored handles that are easy to spot in the garden

Showing Your Tools Some TLC

The simple step of cleaning tools after each use helps keep them free of rust and in good condition to work for you — rather than against you — for years to come. (There's something gratifying about passing Grandma's or Grandpa's tools on to the next generation.)

Giving everything a quick cleaning

Set up a simple cleaning bucket where you store your tools. With everything close at hand, tidying your tools takes just a minute or two. All you need are rags for wiping off dirt and applying lubricant, a stiff brush for scraping off caked mud, and a rust-inhibiting tool lubricant to occasionally wipe on metal parts with a rag after cleaning the tool.

Maintaining wooden handles

Wood will crack, split, or develop splinters if moisture works its way in. Wipe handles dry after use and store your tools out of harm's way from sun, wind, rain, and snow. At the end of your gardening season, spruce up the handle. Use a fine-grit sandpaper to remove splinters. Seal the wood against moisture by wiping it down with a rag dipped in boiled linseed oil, which is available at hardware and home-and-garden stores. Apply multiple coats over a few days to allow the oil to penetrate. This practice can also somewhat rejuvenate an old handle and keep the tool working longer (an especially helpful hint if you find a bargain at a yard or rummage sale).

Chapter 3

The Decomposition Process

*Y*our compost pile is a food web, containing groups of ever-larger inhabitants consuming plant material and each other. Together, they take your kitchen scraps and manure and other stuff and transform it into wonderfully rich growing material. In this chapter, I explain (in not-too-scientific terms) the two major processes — chemical and physical — that break big chunks of raw organic matter into smaller and smaller components that are ultimately used to fuel more cycles of life.

You also get descriptions of the major decomposer organisms in your compost pile. I understand that reading about "bugs" isn't everyone's favorite cup of tea, but I'm willing to bet that you'll get hooked on composting critters sooner or later.

In the meantime, you don't have to understand who is doing what to manage a successful compost system in your backyard. You only have to understand how to keep the decomposers functioning. The last main section of this chapter offers recommendations on managing food, water, air, and temperature to keep your composting actors performing at peak capacity.

Decomp 101: How Rotting Works

Composting critters employ one of two basic methods of decomposition to break down all that debris in your compost pile — chemical or physical. The processes of chemical and physical decomposition are described in the following sections. I also explain how all these composters interact in your compost community.

Going to pieces: The physical breakup

Soil *invertebrates* (creatures lacking backbones) are an amazingly diverse community charged with the endless task of physically reducing mountains of organic refuse to smaller and smaller bits. Depending on species, they attack their work with mouthparts designed for chewing, biting, rasping, shredding, or grinding plant matter.

These varied chomping efforts reduce larger pieces of organic matter into smaller ones with more surface area, which in turn enables bacteria and the other chemical decomposers (which I describe in the next section) to gain a foothold and work more effectively.

Physical decomposers act in the early stages of your compost pile, but as bacterial activity heats up and the temperatures rise, they depart (or die). When temperatures drop back down, you'll notice all sorts of life and movement as physical decomposers return to the pile to continue their work.

Freeing the nutrients: The chemical breakdown

During your compost pile's process of chemical decomposition, microbes such as bacteria and fungi release enzymes that break down complex organic compounds into simpler compounds, which these decomposers can then absorb into their bodies as nutrients. Other organisms obtain nutrients by eating the microbes. And as microbes die, the compounds tied up in their bodies are released and become available for another generation of organisms to use.

No matter how efficiently they work, microbes and other decomposers ultimately reach a point where some substances can't be broken down any further. These byproducts of decomposition become linked together to form *humus,* that most desirable, crumbly, dark brown end result of composting. (Jump back to Chapter 1 to find out more about valuable humus.)

Maintaining balance through the food web

The relationships between members of your compost pile community aren't always friendly, but the organisms — in all their eating and being eaten — contribute to giving you great compost.

A *food chain* depicts what each living organism eats to obtain energy and nutrients, and then, who eats it. The first link is a plant that is consumed by the second link in the chain, perhaps a grasshopper, who is in turn eaten by a quail, and so on. A *food web* depicts a wider community of organisms participating in many interrelated food chains. Your compost pile functions as a hyperactive food web, supporting varied life forms and billions of individuals in their ongoing enterprise of breaking down and recycling organic matter. These diverse organisms create a highly functioning food web by

- ✔ Eating, digesting, and excreting nutrients in forms that other organisms can absorb
- ✔ Regulating populations of organisms so no particular group burgeons out of control
- ✔ Becoming food themselves for higher-level consumers in the food web

Your compost pile's food web always begins with organic residue — leaves, grass clippings, manure, coffee grounds, kitchen scraps, and so on. All that "garbage" you pile up gives life to primary decomposers, who are the first to sit down at the table. They include both physical decomposers and chemical decomposers.

Next up are secondary consumers, organisms that eat primary consumers. Some of these you can spy with the naked eye, such as beetles and springtails. Others are microscopic, including protozoa that eat bacteria.

Tertiary consumers eat secondary consumers. These are the larger (relatively speaking) occupants of your compost pile, such as centipedes and beetles that you can easily see scurrying away when you flip over a mound of organic matter with your fork or shovel.

Table 3-1 groups typical organisms working in your compost pile into levels of primary, secondary, and tertiary consumers.

Table 3-1	Your Compost Pile's Food Web: The Consumers and the Consumed
Consumer Type	*Examples of This Type*
Tertiary consumers (feeding on secondary consumers)	Centipedes, predatory mites, beetles
Secondary consumers (feeding on primary consumers)	Springtails, beetles, mites, nematodes, protozoa
Primary consumers (feeding on organic materials)	Bacteria, actinomycetes, fungi, protozoa, nematodes, sowbugs (woodlice), pillbugs, millipedes, mites, slugs, snails

Who's Doing the Hard Work?

I used to take a break from tossing yet another load of organic matter from one bin into another to lean on my pitchfork, wipe my sweaty brow, survey my accomplishments, and think (somewhat virtuously) that I was "composting." I then had the good fortune to take a Master Composter course and found out that I couldn't lay claim to that effort.

Although I was providing the right conditions for them, it was actually billions and billions (and more billions) of decomposer organisms that were "composting" on my behalf. I don't mind playing second fiddle to this fascinating cast of characters. They play their roles to perfection if I nudge them along just a little, and continue to perform even if I ignore their needs completely.

In the following sections, you get a quick introduction to the critters at work in your compost pile. I discuss the chemical decomposers first — because they do most of the work — and then introduce the physical decomposers. (For more on the difference between physical and chemical decomposition, see the earlier section "Decomp 101: How Rotting Works.") I also toss in some "Fun facts" along the way: Knowing these bits of trivia won't make you any more successful at composting, but they may give you the edge you need to make it big on *Jeopardy!* if you should so aspire.

Counting on chemical decomposers

The specific microbes involved in chemical decomposition — bacteria, actinomycetes, fungi, and protozoa — are the subject of the next sections. I describe them in general order of their population numbers in a typical composting effort.

Bacteria turn up the heat

Bacteria are single-celled organisms. They're the most numerous chemical decomposers, comprising 80 to 90 percent of the microbes working in your pile. They hitch a ride to the compost party on your original ingredients, so the types and numbers of bacteria vary with each pile you construct. The more variety in your ingredients, the more variety in your decomposers, and ultimately, your finished compost will have more nutrients and beneficial characteristics.

Different bacteria thrive at different temperature ranges. When temperatures rise or drop, ruling populations die or become inactive and other species take over to control the action. As bacterial populations thrive — eating, reproducing, and dying — they give off heat as a by-product. You can read more about managing the heat to maximize your composting efforts later in this chapter in the section "Tuning the temperature."

Fun fact: One generation of bacteria in your compost pile lives only 20 to 30 minutes. Kinda gives new meaning to the saying, "So much to do, so little time!"

More bacteria: Actinomycetes get into the act

As earlier bacteria populations consume all the easy-to-break-down compounds, such as simple sugars, actinomycetes (ak-tin-oh-*mahy*-seet-eez) take over to work on complex organic materials such as bark and fibrous or woody stems.

Actinomycetes are single-celled bacteria, although they form long, branching threads or filaments that look more like fungal structures than bacteria. Unlike other types of bacteria in your compost, you can see patches of actinomycetes with the naked eye because they form grayish strands that resemble cobwebs spreading through the outer 4 to 6 inches (10 to 15 centimeters) of a pile.

Fun fact: Your compost's pleasing earthy aroma is produced by actinomycetes releasing gases during the decomposition process.

Fungi fine-tune the process

Like actinomycetes, fungi in your compost pile break down tough organic matter that earlier rounds of decomposers leave behind, such as dry, acidic, or high-carbon materials. Most fungi require less nitrogen than bacteria do, so fungi are important decomposers in piles with high-carbon materials, such as wood chips or sawdust (see "Rationing the carbons and nitrogens" later in this chapter).

Many different fungi types exist in your pile, including microscopic species as well as noticeable, fuzzy, whitish colonies. If you have rotting wood in your pile, you may even see mushrooms sprouting, just as mushrooms cover fallen tree trunks decomposing on a forest floor!

Fun fact: The yeast that's used to bake bread is actually a type of fungi!

Protozoa play along (sort of)

Like bacteria, protozoa are microscopic, one-celled organisms that appear as primary and secondary consumers in your compost. Protozoan populations are far less significant in number — and therefore effectiveness — in your compost pile than the previously described chemical decomposers.

Fun fact: Protozoa are clear and become the same color as what they've just eaten.

Profiting from physical decomposers

Many of the physical decomposers, such as beetles and millipedes, are large enough to easily spot from above. Others, such as mites and springtails, are tiny, although still visible with the naked eye if you scoop up a handful of compost and peer closely. Surprisingly perhaps, the largest population of physical decomposers — *nematodes,* or roundworms — are almost all microscopic so you probably won't see them at work. (However, if you get lucky and notice something that resembles a moving strand of human hair, you're likely observing a nematode.)

I'm going to go out on a limb and declare that if you're reading this book, you're not a soil invertebrate like these other physical decomposers. But if you chop or break organic matter into smaller pieces before mixing it in your pile, you can add yourself to the list of physical decomposers I describe next.

Nematodes (roundworms)

In your compost pile, nematodes, also called roundworms, are worthy allies in your effort to recycle organic matter and nutrients. They consume decaying plant material and eat other decomposers, such as bacteria and fungi.

Tens of thousands of nematode species exist worldwide in every type of environment; there are so many that scientists haven't come close to identifying them all. Depending on species, nematodes are specialized eaters, consuming organic matter, bacteria, fungi, protozoa, and even their destructive (from a human perspective) nematode cousins. (See the earlier section "Counting on chemical decomposers" for more on bacteria and other microbes.)

Fun fact: Nematodes can move through soil only when a film of moisture surrounds soil particles. During dry conditions or drought, nematodes go dormant, reviving when soil moisture is available.

Mites

Mites belong to the class of critters known as arachnids, identified in part by four pairs of legs and no antennae. Like nematodes, the planet is covered with abundant mite species with varying work agendas. Although some mites are notable garden pests (spider mites), many beneficial mites help degrade organic matter in your compost pile. For example, mold mites (also called fermentation mites) feed primarily on yeasts in organic debris. Predatory mites in compost eat varied insects and insect eggs.

Fun fact: Most mold mites have transparent bodies.

Springtails

These intriguing little wingless insects measure from ¹⁄₁₆ inch (1.6 millimeters) up to ¼ inch (6.3 millimeters) in length. They have a hinged, tail-like appendage that bends forward beneath the abdomen and is held in place against the tummy by a "latch." As the latch is released, the appendage "springs" down and launches the insect into the air like a pogo stick. (It's true. I'm not sufficiently imaginative to make that up.)

Because of their jumping motion, springtails are sometimes mistaken for fleas, but they have none of those pests' problem characteristics such as biting or spreading disease. Occasionally, some springtail species may chew on leaves or roots of tender seedlings, although damage is usually insignificant. Established plants are not in any danger from springtails.

Consider any springtails you notice as yet more beneficial occupants of your compost pile, chewing on decomposing plant matter, grains, bacteria, fungi, algae, pollen, and even insect feces. Because moisture and air pass readily through their body surfaces, springtails are highly susceptible to drying out. Thus, you'll most likely spy them in the moister environs of your compost pile.

Fun fact: Springtails "spring" 3 to 4 inches (7.6 to 10 centimeters) in one jump.

Sowbugs and pillbugs

Very similar in appearance, these terrestrial crustaceans breathe with gills, so they require living accommodations that offer moisture and high humidity. You'll likely uncover sowbugs or pillbugs (sometimes called woodlice) in moist areas towards the center or bottom of the compost pile where they feed on decaying plant matter. Although they're not troublesome enough to be labeled as pests, sowbugs and pillbugs may feed on tender living plant tissue, such as young seedlings growing in moist, organically rich soil.

Adults grow up to ⅜-inch (9.5-millimeters) long and have distinct, round body segments and seven pairs of legs. Sowbugs have "tail-like" appendages; pillbugs don't. Without these tails to get in the way, pillbugs roll into tight balls if they feel threatened, which explains another common name enjoyed by kids: "roly-poly."

Fun fact: Sowbugs and pillbugs are related to crayfish, lobster, and shrimp.

Millipedes and centipedes

At first glance, millipedes and centipedes appear similar because they have numerous body segments and legs, but there are many distinctions. Millipedes feed on moist decaying plant matter, helping break down the contents of your compost pile. However, centipedes feed only on living creatures, especially insects and insect larvae. They kill their prey by grasping them and injecting venom. Centipedes may use your compost pile as a hunting ground.

It's generally better to leave millipedes or centipedes untouched in your compost pile, but if you choose to pick them up, wear protective gloves and safety glasses. Centipede bites can be painful, although they're not usually life threatening unless the victim has allergic reactions or is a small child. In such cases, consult your physician or poison control center immediately. Millipedes may eject an irritating fluid that leaves a foul odor, causes skin reactions, and may be harmful if it gets into your eyes. Some species can launch this substance several inches!

Fun fact: Despite their names, millipedes don't sport a thousand legs nor do centipedes stroll about on 100. A more likely leg count is less than 100 for millipedes and about 30 for centipedes.

Beetles

Beetles are hard-shelled insects with two sets of wings folded against their back. Numerous beetle species operate throughout your compost pile, both during their larval life stage (when they're called *grubs*) and as adult beetles. Grubs feed on rotting organic matter. Beetles may consume organic matter but also seek prey such as fly larvae (maggots), mites, and nematodes.

Fun fact: Various beetle species are valuable compost dwellers because they eat the gardener's nemeses — snails and slugs.

Snails and slugs

Snails have protective external spiral shells; slugs are soft-bodied. Otherwise, they exhibit similar characteristics, including the unfortunate ability to decimate your prized vegetable or flowerbed overnight. If you live in humid and/or rainy climates with mild winters where snails and slug populations are prevalent, you're bound to come across them seeking fresh plant debris in your compost pile. You may choose to destroy them because if they — or their eggs — still reside in the finished compost when you spread it around your garden, you've just given them a free pass to the head of the buffet line.

Fun fact: Snails and slugs come out at night, sliding along ground and other surfaces with a broad muscular "foot" that leaves behind a mucus trail. If you don't see these silvery slime trails, you need to track down a different culprit to blame for any plant destruction.

Ants

Most of the physical decomposers in your compost need moist conditions to survive, but ants move in to build nests only if conditions are fairly dry. They'll depart if you thoroughly moisten the pile and/or cook it up to high temperatures.

Abundant ant activity is a sign that your organic matter is too dry for speedy decomposition, which may or may not matter to you.

Most ants are beneficial in a compost pile, eating all kinds of stuff, including fungi, food scraps, seeds, and even other ants. They also help develop richer compost by transporting important minerals such as phosphorous and potassium from one area to another.

Fun fact: Ants can lift 20 times their own weight.

Flies

Flies are two-winged insects that are seldom problematic with a compost pile. Adult flies feed on organic material and deposit their eggs in compost piles to provide a ready food source for hatching larvae (maggots). Maggots, in turn, are eaten by mites and other creatures, so it's all part of the food web.

If maggot populations seem out-of-control (or just gross you out), heat up your pile — high temperature ranges kill fly larvae.

If you experience problems with airborne pests, such as houseflies or horseflies, buzzing around your compost pile, get out your pitchfork, because your pile needs attention. Properly tended compost doesn't attract flies. Check out the advice in Chapter 5 on pest control.

Fun fact: Flies are said to carry over 1,941,000 different kinds of bacteria, some of which will end up in your compost pile to break down organic matter.

Earthworms

Earthworms are the ultimate composting machines, consuming and digesting organic matter to deposit their rich waste, called *casts* or *castings.* Earthworms are so important to the planet's recycling of organic matter and soil building, as well as your composting efforts, that they deserve their own chapter. Jump ahead to Chapter 10 to read about these incredible creatures.

Fun fact: Although worms have no eyes, they can sense light.

A cozy home for wildlife

As well as all the creatures that take an active part in the composting process, a compost heap is the ultimate happy home for other kinds of creatures — mostly beneficial ones that do gardeners a good turn. The warm, cozy, dark environment is a great place for frogs, toads, lizards, and newts — even slowworms and hedgehogs — especially in winter when it's cold outside, so take great care to look out for all these little chaps when turning or emptying your heap.

Creating a Productive Work Environment

Preceding sections in this chapter provide an overview of the major players in your compost pile. It's fun stuff to know, but you don't need to memorize the names of organisms to help them work efficiently. Simply create and maintain a hospitable living environment for them. Their requirements for life are similar to yours and mine: food, water, air, and appropriate temperature. The remainder of this chapter explains the best way to provide ongoing life support to your composting critters.

Rationing the carbons and nitrogens

All organic matter you add to your compost pile contains carbon and nitrogen in its tissues. The amounts vary widely, as the table "Carbon to Nitrogen Ratios" in Chapter 7 depicts.

Most decomposers guzzling organic matter in your compost pile prefer a diet that contains 30 times as much carbon as nitrogen (C:N), or 30:1. They use carbon-rich material for energy and nitrogen-rich material for building cells. The closer you come to mixing that ideal ratio with your ingredients, the more efficiently the organisms can make use of it — and the faster you obtain useable compost.

If there is considerably more carbon than nitrogen (for example, cardboard has a ratio of 600:1), numerous generations of organisms must plow through that carbon, die to free up the limited nitrogen already in their bodies for the next generation of decomposers to use, and so on. The composting process continues as the limited nitrogen is recycled, but it would occur much faster if the ingredients' ratios were closer to 30:1 from the start.

Too much carbon slows things down, but too much nitrogen has its own unpleasant effect. If you have, for example, a mountain of grass clippings at 25:1 without carbons to mix with it, odor problems are not far behind. Because decomposers don't have carbon to go with all that nitrogen as they work through it, excess nitrogen is lost to the atmosphere as smelly ammonia gas.

An easy way to juggle the ratios provided in Chapter 7's table for an approximate balance is to use 3 parts carbon materials to 1 part nitrogen materials by volume. In other words, 3 carts full of brown stuff mixed with 1 cart full of green stuff. Another option is a 50-50 mix of brown to green. Don't get bogged down in numbers; composting will still take place at other ratios, so don't worry about precision. With time, you'll develop mixes of ingredients that perform well for you.

Sizing down particles

In Chapter 8's step-by-step instructions on building a basic compost pile, I recommend chopping up most ingredients into small pieces. I also mention that you don't need complete uniformity with only tiny bits, because some larger chunks enhance aeration. Keep in mind that for the majority of your ingredients, the smaller the pieces of organic matter, the faster the rate of decomposition because

- ✔ Plant materials' defense mechanisms against invasion by microbes are weakened by cuts, scrapes, and wounds from chopping and shredding.

- ✔ More surface area is created with lots and lots of small pieces. Increased surface area allows chemical and physical decomposers more avenues of attack.

- ✔ When building your pile, smaller, uniform pieces with lots of surface area are easier to moisten thoroughly.

- ✔ Uniform materials are easier to turn and remoisten.

- ✔ Uniform materials self-insulate and heat up faster to create a hot pile (more on that coming up in "Tuning the temperature").

How small is small enough? Reduce the bulk of your organic matter into 2-inch-long (5-centimeter) bits and pieces.

Managing moisture and air

Moisture and aeration are often discussed as separate issues in composting, but I find it's helpful to consider them together because your actions to manage water and air in the compost pile are closely linked.

Billions of pore spaces surround the organic particles in your compost. Pores allow air and water to circulate through the compost ingredients. If there's insufficient moisture, the decomposer organisms close up shop. On the other hand, if pores are flooded with water, airflow is hindered, and you're stuck with a smelly anaerobic (without air) compost pile to deal with. (Read more about the differences between aerobic and anaerobic composting in Chapter 4.)

Your goal is to balance moisture and air levels to optimize conditions for the decomposers, thereby maximizing your composting efforts. Here's what you need to know.

Maintaining enough moisture

The organisms I describe earlier in this chapter require moisture to survive. Most of them perform their decomposing magic in ultra-thin films of water on the surface of organic particles. When your pile's moisture level drops below 35 to 40 percent and materials dry out, most of the creatures die or go dormant.

The ideal moisture content for your compost pile is 40 to 60 percent by weight. Nope, there's no need to weigh anything! An easy method to judge moisture content is to squeeze a few handfuls of materials from different areas of the pile. Everything should feel damp, like a wrung-out sponge. If it doesn't, it's time to add water.

You can help preserve existing moisture in your open compost pile by covering it with a tarp.

Having too much of a good thing: Drowning out air

On the other hand, soggy materials handicap your composting. Moisture content above 65 to 70 percent blocks air flow and develops into stinky anaerobic conditions. Nutrients also leach out of overly wet compost piles. If you can squeeze more than a drop or two of water out of a handful of ingredients, the pile is too wet.

Pore spaces in the pile provide essential oxygen for the survival of composting organisms. Pores also allow for the escape of carbon dioxide, which is a by-product of their decomposing efforts. Adequate aeration also helps maintain high temperatures, which produce faster rates of decomposition and kill weed seeds and pathogens. (Pile temperatures are covered in an upcoming section.)

If you live in extremely rainy regions, covering your pile helps prevent it from turning soggy during a deluge.

Finding the perfect balance

Fine-tune your pile's moisture and air levels by:

✔ Turning the organic matter to introduce more air and/or dry out wet materials. A properly aerated pile has no bad odors. If it smells, it's likely too wet and needs to be turned!

✔ Adding dry carbon materials, such as leaves, straw, or saw- dust, to soak up excess moisture.

✔ Rewetting materials if they dry out, usually at the same time you turn the pile.

Tuning the temperature

Most decomposing action in your compost pile occurs within two temperature ranges — mesophilic and thermophilic — with differ- ent organisms thriving in each.

Mesophilic critters function from about 40 to 104 degrees Fahrenheit (4 to 40 degrees Celsius), although they're most pro- ductive in your compost pile from 70 to 90 degrees Fahrenheit (21 to 32 degrees Celsius). Mesophilic bacteria get busy initially on the easy-to-decompose materials, such as simple soluble sugars. They generate heat as a by-product of their frenzied eating, reproduc- ing, and dying, which causes your compost pile's temperature to rise. Unable to operate at higher temperatures, the mesophiles are usurped by thermophiles.

Thermophilic organisms thrive from 105 to 140 degrees Fahrenheit (41 to 60 degrees Celsius), although some can function up to 175 degrees Fahrenheit (79 degrees Celsius). During this hot phase, these heat-tolerant microorganisms start breaking down the tough stuff, such as complex carbohydrates.

Understanding a thermophilic compost pile

Although usually labeled as the thermophilic composting method (or "hot" composting), this process also contains two phases of mesophilic decomposition that sandwich the middle hot phase (see Figure 3-1):

1. **Phase 1:** Mesophilic (medium temperature) microorgan- isms and soil invertebrates start the process.

   Initial temperature ranges in a compost pile vary depend- ing on its ingredients, overall size, moisture, and aeration, as well as your geographic region. As a general guideline, a well-constructed pile's initial temperature runs about 50 to 70 degrees Fahrenheit (10 to 21 degrees Celsius) and rises rapidly within one to five days. Mesophilic decomposers dominate up to 104 degrees Fahrenheit (40 degrees Celsius).

The more ideal your mix of carbon to nitrogen ingredients, particle size, moisture, and air (see earlier sections for more on these components), the faster the pile will heat, sometimes within hours.

2. **Phase 2:** Thermophilic (high temperature) microorganisms take over at 105 degrees Fahrenheit (41 degrees Celsius).

   Depending on the same pile characteristics listed in Phase 1, as well as additional turning to increase aeration and remoistening as needed, temperatures jump quickly to 120 degrees Fahrenheit (49 degrees Celsius) and may even reach 150 degrees Fahrenheit (66 degrees Celsius) or more.

   As temperatures drop slightly after a few days, turning to provide more airflow causes temperatures to climb again. When the supply of favored foods is used up, thermophilic microbial activity declines, and the pile temperature drops.

3. **Phase 3:** Mesophilic creatures reassert control as temperatures drop below 104 degrees Fahrenheit (40 degrees Celsius).

   In addition to microorganisms that thrive in these temperatures, soil invertebrates that physically decompose plant material begin repopulating the pile. This final decomposition phase can last weeks or months, depending on how long you let your compost "cure" before you use it. Temperature in the pile typically matches the surrounding air temperatures.

Managing the heat

Understanding these temperature phases and managing a thermophilic compost pile helps you to produce useable compost quickly. All materials eventually break down in cool, unmanaged compost piles as well, but decomposition occurs faster with higher temperatures. Also, if you need to destroy weed seeds or plant pathogens during the composting process, creating a hot, thermophilic pile is essential.

Following are tips for working with a hot pile:

- ✔ **Take its temperature:** Use a compost thermometer (see Chapter 2) to take your pile's temperature daily. Record it in a notebook or spreadsheet, and over time you'll get a feel for how long different phases take with your composting ingredients and methods.

- ✔ **Size it right:** Compost piles require mass to self-insulate and maintain high temperatures during thermophilic composting. The minimum size is 3 x 3 x 3 feet (1 cubic yard or 1 cubic meter) up to 5 x 5 x 5 feet (1.5 cubic meters). This size allows the material to self-insulate and is easy to turn for a typical gardener. Larger sizes inhibit airflow to the center of the pile.

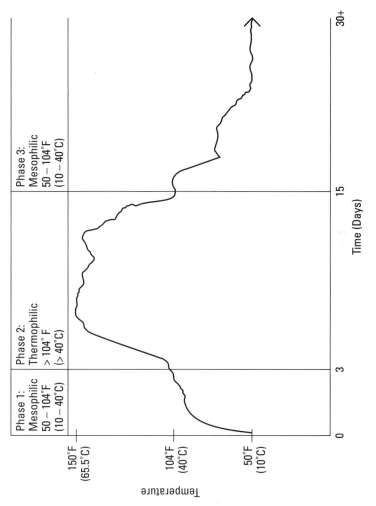

Figure 3-1: Three phases of thermophilic composting.

✔ **Turn, mix, and water:** Temperatures drop as supplies of food, air, and water are exhausted. Turning the pile to aerate, mixing undecomposed ingredients on the outside into the center, and/or adding moisture may encourage temperatures to rise and promote more rapid decomposition. At some point, food supplies are exhausted and turning the pile no longer boosts temperatures.

✔ **Destroy pathogens and weed seeds:** Most plant pathogens are destroyed if temperatures remain between 130 and 140 degrees Fahrenheit (54 to 60 degrees Celsius) for 72 hours. Most weed seeds are destroyed if exposed to temperatures above 131 degrees Fahrenheit (55 degrees Celsius) for 72 hours. (Chapter 8 provides details on cooking up a hot pile to destroy weed seeds and plant pathogens.)

✔ **Don't overheat:** Heating your pile above 170 degrees Fahrenheit (77 degrees Celsius) for more than a few hours is not recommended, because it inhibits most microbial activity and shuts down the decomposition process.

If the pile is too hot, turn it to aerate the core and release heat build-up.

Part II

Selecting a Home and Method for Your Compost

The 5th Wave   By Rich Tennant

"...and here's where we threw all our trash, like coffee grounds, egg shells, romance novels..."

In this part . . .

This part helps you sort out the best location and style for your composting endeavors, starting with composting at its most basic — in a freestanding pile or in a hole dug in the ground. It also covers the difference between aerobic and anaerobic composting methods and why it matters to you.

This part also addresses your compost container options. First I sort out the advantages and disadvantages of container styles and provide advice you can use if you decide to purchase one; I also describe kitchen composter options for folks who don't have outdoor space for a traditional compost system. The part closes with step-by-step instructions for numerous compost containers that you can build. Most of them are simple and can be made from recycled materials at little or no expense.

Chapter 4

Composting Aboveground or Underground: No Bin Required

. . . .

In This Chapter

▶ Composting in a pile or in a pit

▶ Understanding aerobic and anaerobic decomposition

. . . .

I wear a T-shirt that proclaims: Compost Happens. Because compost really does seem to "just happen," it's also a simple skill to learn, as this chapter explains. Heap up material in a freestanding pile or bury your kitchen scraps. Voilá! You're officially a composter. This chapter also explains the differences between aerobic (with air) and anaerobic (without air) decomposition and provides basic steps to perform both types.

Composting Without a Container

Composting without the confines of a container takes place in two basic ways: aboveground in a freestanding pile or below ground in a hole.

Freestanding piles are just that: heaps of organic matter piled up without an enclosure to corral them. Underground composting, better known as *pit* or *trench composting,* involves digging a hole, throwing in your stuff, and covering it up with soil.

Following are the advantages and disadvantages associated with no-bin composting. If you decide that neither option suits you, jump ahead to Chapter 5.

No-bin composting is particularly advantageous under the following circumstances:

✔ If you want to try your hand at composting with as little expense as possible, it doesn't get much cheaper than a pile of leaves and grass clippings or a hole in the ground loaded with kitchen scraps! You can gain experience with these methods, and then decide whether you want to "upgrade" to a container.

✔ If you have lots of yard space and elbowroom, freestanding piles are fine. (It also helps if you don't have looky-loo neighbors to peer with dismay upon your mounds of organic matter.)

✔ If you have lots and lots and lots and lots of organic matter, larger freestanding piles called *windrows* may suit you. Refer to the sidebar "Working with windrows" for more on this.

✔ If your ground is easy to dig, trench composting is a viable option.

✔ If you want to dispose of kitchen scraps without attracting pests, trench composting does the trick (see the later section, "Keeping Your Binless Compost Critter-Free" for more info).

✔ If you want to compost at the site of future planting areas, either method is good, and you don't have to move containers around from year to year.

Of course, no-bin composting has its downsides, too. They include the following:

✔ Sprawling piles of organic matter may appear messy, unless, of course, you like to observe big piles of leaves, grass, and plant trimmings shrink into smaller piles of chocolate-brown compost. (Beauty is in the eye of the beholder.)

✔ Although you may do your best to maintain a tidy area, there's no reliable way to keep pests out of freestanding piles. Rodents, raccoons, dogs, foxes, badgers, and others may gladly root around in search of something tasty to eat. (See the later section "Keeping Your Binless Compost Critter-Free" for more on this.)

✔ If your ground is hard, rocky, and difficult to dig, you'd have to be crazy to choose trench composting on a regular basis. Crazy!

An Issue of Air: Aerobic versus Anaerobic Composting

Two broad categories of microorganisms consume and decompose organic matter: *aerobic* (those that need air) and *anaerobic* (those that don't). This section helps you to understand how these microorganisms work and guides you in determining which type of composting is best suited to your style.

Aerobic composting: Keeping everything aboveground

Most folks who compost do so aboveground. It's the simplest method to start with because all that's required is a pile of organic matter. Aerobic composting is the principle at work in aboveground composting environments — whether it takes place in a freestanding pile or in a container that provides air circulation, such as a bin with open sides or a tumbler with aeration holes (you can see these bins in Chapter 5).

Air is the most essential ingredient in aerobic composting. If you've ever jumped and thumped through an aerobic exercise class and found yourself gasping for air, you know firsthand that oxygen is required to work out at maximum capacity. The same principle applies to aerobic organisms in your compost pile — oxygen is key to optimum performance.

Making sure aerobic organisms get enough air

As long as plenty of air is available, aerobic decomposers work faster and more efficiently than their anaerobic counterparts, providing you with finished compost on a faster timetable. However, as organisms deplete the supply of oxygen from the existing spaces and pores between bits of organic matter, the decomposition process slows.

To keep your decomposers working at maximum speed, you may want to incorporate some type of aeration aid during your initial pile construction. One way to do this is to pile organic materials on top of a recycled shipping pallet. The pallet sits several inches above the ground's surface, allowing air to flow beneath it. Chapter 8 describes other methods you can employ when you're building your pile to enhance airflow for aerobic decomposers.

Continue to monitor your pile's progress, and make adjustments as necessary. If you notice the height of your compost pile shrinking (it may shrink as much as a foot within a few days of its initial construction), you can reenergize your aerobicizers by giving your pile a fresh infusion of oxygen. You can accomplish this in a couple ways:

- ✔ **Turn your pile completely.** Fork a freestanding heap to an adjacent spot or turn the contents of one bin into another. If using a tumbler, give it a spin.

- ✔ **Stir organic matter regularly.** Use a pitchfork or an aerating tool to stir things up (Chapter 2 describes these tools). You may want to do this daily for maximum results.

It's not unusual to find pockets of anaerobic composting going on within an aboveground pile that's meant to be aerobic-only. If your compost is emitting a bad odor, like rotten eggs or ammonia, it's too wet or too "green" with a thick, moist layer of grass clippings, fresh manure, or other nitrogen-rich organic matter that wasn't thoroughly mixed with dry, carbon-rich materials, such as leaves or straw. These impenetrable masses don't allow air to flow through, and anaerobic organisms are ready and willing to take over.

In addition to being unpleasant to work around, noxious compost odors may annoy neighbors, so head off potential problems by mixing up your initial batch of compost with appropriate amounts of carbon and nitrogen ingredients. If your pile emits odors, review the troubleshooting tips in Chapter 14, which can help you correct any malodorous compost adventures.

Reaping the rewards of warmth and nature's perfume

Aboveground aerobic decomposers can withstand higher temperatures than their anaerobic counterparts, and they generate heat as a by-product of their activity. Not all aboveground piles are "hot," but when conditions are to the decomposers' liking (as described in Chapter 3), temperatures in your pile heat up sufficiently to kill weed seeds and pathogens.

Perhaps the most potent characteristic of aerobic composting is that it's a sweet-smelling project. A well-constructed compost pile doesn't smell bad. In fact, it emits a refreshing earthy aroma, like kicking up leaves during a walk through the woods. Specialized aerobic bacteria called *actinomycetes* emit that agreeable smell as a byproduct of their decomposing actions. (You can read more about actinomycetes in Chapter 3.)

Anaerobic decomposition: Working without air underground

Anaerobic organisms work without oxygen, so most anaerobic composting (at least the kind that's done on purpose) takes place underground in pits or trenches. (That's why common names for anaerobic composting include *trench composting* or *pit composting*.) Basically, you dig a hole, fill it with organic matter, and seal it with a layer of soil. Anaerobic decomposers get right to work, with no need for fresh O_2 infusions from you.

When anaerobic composting is beneficial

Anaerobic organisms work at slower rates than their aerobic counterparts, and it's impossible to monitor their progress without digging into the hole and poking around. Unfortunately, this can be an odious encounter! Anaerobic organisms, unlike the sweet-smelling actinomycetes I describe earlier, exude smelly gas as a by-product of their exertions. And because they work in colder conditions, weed seeds and plant pathogens aren't destroyed.

Despite these disadvantages, in some situations anaerobic composting is the best way to go. It may suit you if any of the following apply:

✔ You're looking to dispose of a one-time load of wet, potentially smelly, or pest-attracting kitchen waste, such as you'd accumulate after a day spent canning fruits or vegetables, cleaning freshly caught fish, or organizing a big social gathering that generates food scraps.

Dig a hole in advance of the event and you'll be all set to dispose of waste. Paper napkins and plates can go in with the food scraps!

✔ Pulling spent garden plants at the end of fall leaves you with an enormous pile of organic matter that you don't have the space or time to manage over winter.

✔ Aboveground composting of kitchen scraps without a sealed container isn't allowed where you live.

✔ You aren't keen on the appearance of a compost area in your landscape, but you prefer not to send your organic waste to a landfill.

✔ You want to improve soil structure and fertility in a future garden bed.

✔ You don't have time to monitor the air or moisture requirements of — let alone turn — an aboveground compost pile.

Converting an anaerobic pile to an aerobic one

A weekend composting demonstration at my county cooperative extension office proved to be an example of the potency of anaerobic composting. A local landscaper had agreed to drop a load of fresh-cut grass clippings, but unfortunately, the truckload arrived on Monday rather than Friday. The enormous mountain of clippings languished all week in the sun without benefit of turning or mixing with other materials. By Saturday, when the volunteers arrived to learn about composting, this steaming, reeking pile illustrated all sorts of important principles!

Anaerobic creatures jump into action when materials are too wet, too compressed, and/or there's a lack of air circulation — all problems exhibited by the grass mountain. However, the volunteers learned that amending such a problem isn't difficult. They cheerfully and thoroughly mixed the clippings with three times as much dry, carbon-rich materials, such as leaves, shredded paper, and straw. The mixing and turning processes incorporated oxygen and soaked up excess moisture. Within a day or so, the odors dissipated, and the newly constructed compost piles were decomposing nicely.

Taking the hardness of the ground into account

I think that becoming an anaerobic composting convert depends on where you live and how easy it is to dig holes in the ground. I'm a desert gardener where the ground is hard, rocky, compacted, and might even offer an impervious hardpan layer just to show the gardener who's boss. I dig a planting hole over a period of days, because I soak the soil with water and scrape out a few inches of soil at a time, employing a well-worn pick ax. Voluntarily digging more holes just to throw in rotting organic matter is not something I can muster any enthusiasm for!

On the other hand, I have an arid-land gardener friend who practices anaerobic composting in her garden beds, where the improved soil is loose and easy to work with. She digs a hole, tucks in her day's worth of kitchen scraps, and covers it up. She doesn't want to retrieve useable compost, but allows the organic matter to rot in place to improve her garden beds over time.

Creating a Pile Aboveground

Creating a freestanding pile is the easiest method to break into composting. This section covers the basics to give you an idea of the process. Refer to Chapter 9 for complete step-by-step instructions (and to understand the whys behind them) for building compost piles.

Where to site the pile

Location is everything according to realtors, and so it is with your compost pile. An ideal spot is shady (so materials don't dry out), doesn't get inundated with rain (so materials don't get soggy), and within reach of your hose. It should offer sufficient space for you to work comfortably. Compost at least a few feet away from buildings so moisture from the pile doesn't seep into foundations.

Aboveground composting in a few simple steps

Build a freestanding pile at least 3 feet x 3 feet x 3 feet (1 cubic yard or 1 cubic meter) up to 5 cubic feet (1.5 cubic meters). This size offers enough mass for the organic matter to self-insulate and maintain moisture and warmth for the microorganisms consuming it.

Chop, shred, or break as much of your organic matter as possible into small pieces. The smaller the pieces, the faster the rate of decomposition. See Chapter 7 for a list of compostable *brown* (carbon-rich) and *green* (nitrogen-rich) ingredients to add to your pile. Follow these basic steps to create your pile:

1. **Spread 4 inches (10 centimeters) of woody, chunky, or coarse brown ingredients, such as straw, corn stalks, or dead perennial stems, as your pile's base.**

   This rough layer promotes aeration.

2. **Sprinkle each layer with water as you build the pile so that it has the dampness of a wrung-out sponge. Also sprinkle in a few handfuls (or shovelfuls) of native soil here and there (you don't have to add soil with every layer).**

3. **Spread 4 to 5 more inches (10 to 13 centimeters) of brown materials, such as dry leaves or shredded paper.**

4. **Spread 2 to 3 inches (5 to 8 centimeters) of green materials, such as spent garden plants and grass clippings.**

5. **Continue alternating layers of browns and greens, moistening as you build. Finish up with a layer of browns on top.**

Working with windrows

Windrow composting is a style typically used by farmers to process animal waste, straw bedding, and crop residue in long, narrow rows that are turned with specialized equipment. The same requirements of composting in small piles (carbon and nitrogen materials, moisture, and aeration) apply.

You can adapt windrow composting if you have sufficient space and lots of organic matter to process. Stack your materials 3 to 5 feet (1 to 1.5 meters) high and wide, in rows as long as you need them to be. The drawback with windrows is, of course, the effort involved in turning all that stuff by hand! If you plan to windrow compost on a regular basis, you may want to use a compact tractor or front-end loader. You can also let the organic matter sit without turning to decompose more slowly.

You have the option of covering the pile with a tarp. It helps keep materials from drying out in arid regions. In rainy climates, it prevents the pile from getting too wet and turning anaerobic.

When your compost will be ready to use

The length of time needed to obtain finished compost varies depending on how you mix up the original elements (types of ingredients, size of particles, and moisture levels) and how much turning and remoistening you choose to do after the pile is built.

If you're in no hurry for compost, you can leave the pile sit as is. However, to jumpstart the decomposition process, add a fresh burst of oxygen as needed (see the earlier section "Making sure aerobic organisms get enough air" for details). Turn the compost to mix materials on the outside of the pile into the interior so everything decomposes at a similar rate.

If you do nothing further after building your pile, in three to six months you'll be able to harvest some finished compost from the bottom and center. Further decomposition (without turning or moistening) can take a year or more. Average decomposition time to obtain considerable finished compost from a "well-constructed" pile (as I describe in Chapter 8) that is regularly turned and remoistened is about two to three months. Chapter 8 includes complete details for building piles to obtain compost results in various timeframes.

Digging a Hole (Pit or Trench Composting)

If you live where digging holes in the ground is no big deal (lucky you), the following info helps you add anaerobic composting to your repertoire.

Where to site the hole

Because appearance isn't an issue as it might be with aboveground composting, you can trench compost just about anywhere that's convenient and easy for you to dig. Be sure you know where underground utility lines run before digging. Good choices to consider include areas where you want to add a future flower, vegetable, or herb garden, or between rows of existing garden beds. Avoid marshy areas or low spots with wet soil or poor drainage.

Stay away from existing root systems when digging composting holes. Tree and shrub roots easily expand to twice the diameter of their aboveground canopy! Slicing through roots with a shovel creates easy wounds for pests and diseases to enter, ultimately weakening and possibly killing your plant. If you're unsure how far roots may have spread, stick to digging compost trenches in garden beds.

Pit composting in a few simple steps

Depending upon what you want to achieve, you can employ several different methods of pit or trench composting, such as digging random holes, filling trench rows in garden beds, or rotating trenches over a three-year period to improve an expanded planting area. Use the basic anaerobic trench compost recipe that follows for whichever method you choose.

Fill 'er up

How deep and wide to dig depends on how much organic matter you have to compost, what kind of material it is (landscape waste versus kitchen waste), how easy it is to dig, and whether digging pests might be an issue (see the section "Keeping Your Binless Compost Critter-Free" for more on the latter).

If you want to eventually retrieve finished compost from your pit, realize that the deeper it is, the more cumbersome it is to remove. Scooping out finished compost from long, shallow trenches that are 1 to 2 feet (30 to 60 centimeters) deep is easier than retrieving it from deeper holes with steep sides.

1. **Dig the hole or trench, reserving the soil that you remove.**

2. **Follow the earlier instructions for aerobic composting. Starting with browns on the bottom, alternate layers of brown and green materials, moistening as you build.**

   Spread a 1-inch (2.5-centimeter) layer of your reserved soil between layers of browns and greens.

3. **Cover with 4 to 8 inches (10 to 20 centimeters) of soil. If you plan to retrieve the compost later, mark the area with a stone or other reminder.**

Placing trenches between garden rows

If you grow flowers, herbs, or vegetables in straight rows with plenty of space between them, dig and fill composting trenches between the rows. As the organic matter in the trenches decomposes, nutrients become available for nearby plants. Dig trenches early in the planting season before vigorous roots expand into the area. Alternatively, dig trenches at the end of your growing season, so material is decomposed by the next planting season.

Preparing trenches for hungry crops

Certain plants really thrive on soil that's rich in organic matter and water-holding material, particularly sweet peas, runner beans, zucchini (courgettes in the United Kingdom), pumpkins, and squash.

Six to eight months before planting, dig a trench or pit where you plan to grow these crops, 18 inches (45 centimeters) deep. Fill with kitchen waste, newspaper, manure, and other retentive materials, then top with a 6-inch (15-centimeter) layer of soil, heaping it up to form a mound. By the time your planting season rolls around, the site will have settled and be ready for seeds or transplants.

Rotating trenches with planting areas

This method helps you develop good garden soil over time by rotating trench composting areas with planting areas and pathways that allow access to your plants.

Divide the gardening space into three equal areas: one for growing plants, one for pathways to access the plants, and one for trench composting. Each year, you can plant in the previous year's trench, and shift the other areas accordingly, as shown in Figure 4-1.

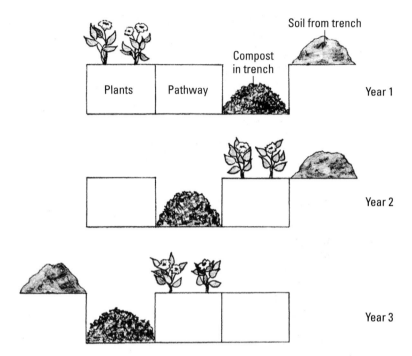

Figure 4-1: Three-year plan for rotating trench composting with planting areas.

At the end of the three years, you'll have improved soil in the entire location and be ready to repeat the process. Organic matter in the soil disappears through the action of decomposer organisms, so it needs constant replenishment.

This method also helps you with a recommended gardening practice called *crop rotation*, in which annual vegetables and flowers are deliberately grown in different locales in the garden — or rotated — each season to prevent build-up of soil-borne pests and diseases.

When your compost will be ready to use

The speed of decomposition underground depends on factors similar to those applicable to aboveground decomposition, such as the ingredient mix, size of particles, and moisture level. The process may take anywhere from several months to a year or more.

Trench composting in winter

If you garden in cold climates and plan to trench compost kitchen waste through the winter, dig a hole in fall before the ground freezes. Keep the removed soil close at hand in a pile. Cover the pile with a thick layer of straw, manure, dried leaves, or sod to insulate it as much as possible from freezing solid so you can dig into it as needed.

Layer the bottom of the hole with four to six inches of brown carbon materials, such as leaves or straw. Cover the hole with a sturdy tarp or slab of plywood to keep snow out. Add kitchen scraps throughout winter, sprinkling some of the reserved soil over new additions.

Keeping Your Binless Compost Critter-Free

Actually, that header is a tad misleading. If you're composting aboveground in a freestanding pile, I'm not aware of any surefire methods to keep pests at bay if they decide to visit (assuming you aren't going to surround your compost area with an electric fence and stand guard 24/7). The best deterrent is to keep kitchen scraps out of freestanding piles. Even without scraps, some higher-ups on the food chain may be drawn to succulent grubs or other insects that inhabit the later stages of your rotting organic matter.

If you want to compost kitchen scraps without building or buying an enclosed bin (read more about that possibility in Chapter 5), burying them to decompose anaerobically is an option. Discourage digging pests from uprooting your tasty scraps by covering the organic matter with a top layer of soil at least 6 inches (15 centimeters) thick (8 inches [20 centimeters] is preferable), adjusting the depth of your hole to accommodate that top layer. Alternatively, cover the organic matter with something heavy that pests can't push aside, such as a boulder, layer of bricks, or shipping pallet. Spreading a section of hardware cloth, chain link fencing, or poultry wire over the hole is another option — animals don't like to get their feet and claws stuck in wire.

Chapter 5

Working with Compost Containers

A great thing about the composting process is that there are so many different ways to do it. As I explain in Chapter 4, you can opt for a free-standing compost heap or one buried underground. Or you can opt for a compost container for a more . . . well, contained . . . approach.

This chapter covers everything you need to know about composting containers, starting with helping you decide whether containers are right for your situation and then covering the pros and cons of tumblers and bins. I give you ideas for choosing among kitchen composters (designed to handle everyday food scraps) and discuss how to deal with wildlife that visits your composting operation. The chapter concludes with characteristics to mull over when buying a manufactured compost container.

Composting in a Container (Or Two or Three)

Mother Nature doesn't enclose her organic debris in containers, yet aromatic black *humus* — the beneficial result of her successful composting process — covers forest floors. Why should you buy or build a container to corral your composting efforts? Truthfully, you don't have to. Freestanding piles perform the job just fine, as Chapter 4 describes, and no particular difference exists between organic matter rotting in a heap and organic matter rotting in a container. However, as you discover in this section, there are reasons why confining organic matter to its quarters may be beneficial to you.

When using containers is best

Acceptable landscape aesthetics vary widely by individual, neighborhood, and community standards. If you're fortunate to live where local government encourages home composting to reduce solid waste sent to landfills, you may be surrounded by supportive neighbors who also compost. (I like to envision the day when composting replaces cars as the new "keeping up with the Jones's" behavior: "Honey, the neighbors added a third bin. Get out there and build us another!")

On the other hand, you may be surrounded by those who are less enthusiastic and don't want to see your mounds of organic matter from their backyard or windows. Using containers that hide organic matter with fully enclosed sides or containers that you can tuck discretely into out-of-view locations forestalls potential complaints.

Other good reasons to employ containers in your composting efforts include the following:

- ✔ Containers keep your stockpiles of dried materials, such as leaves, straw, and sawdust, under control until you need them. Without some type of holding unit, your carefully collected ingredients might end up scattered around the yard the next time a mighty wind blows through.

- ✔ Keeping kitchen scraps in and pests out is another important benefit offered by containers that are completely enclosed and feature secure lids. Read "Keeping Wildlife Out of Your Container" later in the chapter for more details.

- ✔ When it comes to efficient composting, maintaining the overall size and shape of your original pile of ingredients is easier within the confines of containers. When compost materials have sufficient mass (at least 1 cubic yard [1 cubic meter], as explained in Chapter 4), they're better able to self-insulate to maintain consistent moisture levels and higher temperatures, conditions that speed decomposition.

- ✔ Fully enclosed bins help organic matter retain moisture, a characteristic that's useful if you live in an arid climate. Decomposition slows down when the compost pile dries out.

- ✔ If you live in a rainy climate, enclosed bins keep heavy rains from soaking organic matter. Wet piles turn anaerobic and smelly (see Chapter 4 for details on anaerobic composting).

- ✔ Some bins offer insulating qualities that help increase and maintain higher temperatures inside.

Sorting out your composting style

Because I mention at the start of this chapter that you don't need a container to generate compost and you're still reading, I assume that you've decided a container makes sense for you. The questions in this section help you start sorting out your options to find the best container for your particular needs.

How much money do you want to spend?

Many styles of manufactured containers are showing up in the marketplace as the concepts of green living, sustainability, and composting gain in popularity. Contemplate the advantages and disadvantages of the manufactured containers I include later in this chapter to decide whether their price tag is reasonable for your budget.

 You don't have to purchase an expensive container to get started. There are many container possibilities you can produce quite easily (even if you're not handy with tools) using recycled materials, such as 55-gallon, plastic, food-grade drums with tight-fitting lids. Drill drainage holes in the bottom or cut the bottom off completely, which also makes it easy to pick up the drum and set it aside when it's time to turn or harvest compost. Chapter 6 covers other inexpensive options and provides step-by-step building instructions.

How much organic matter will you process?

You may have moved into a new home and want to start a garden, but you have no idea how much organic matter your landscape and household will produce. Or you may have bagged copious quantities of grass clippings all summer and then switched to raking mountains of leaves in autumn (and paid to have your trash disposal company haul it all away, depending on where you live), and you have a good estimate of the amount of organic matter your household generates.

Whatever your situation, it may help you to think of composting in containers as a "modular" system. If you're uncertain how much organic matter you'll have, start off with a single square bin from the options I describe in Chapter 6, such as concrete blocks, shipping pallets, or even straw bales. As you gain experience and get bitten by the compost "bug," you can easily expand your operation. The square shape makes it a snap to add a second or third adjacent bin. The three-bin composting method is perfect for processing a lot of organic matter (see the section "Bins of all types" later in this chapter).

How much space do you have for a composting area?

Check out possible areas in your landscape, and estimate whether containers will fit in the areas you're thinking about. Factor in elbow room for comfortable movement, including turning the pile by hand or filling a wheelbarrow or cart with finished compost.

Some local governments or homeowner's associations may have restrictions on composting activities, such as "no kitchen scraps aboveground" or "bins can't be seen from the street." Although a three-bin system made from shipping pallets may stand out, there are other options that you can tuck into an out-of-sight corner. I also offer a variety of methods for disposing of kitchen scraps in the section "Kitchen composters" later in the chapter.

Checking Out Your Options

This section describes characteristics of different container styles, including tumblers, bins, and kitchen composters. There are numerous options to suit different situations. If something here doesn't catch your eye, get busy on the drawing board inventing a new style!

Taking a turn with tumblers

Soil organisms decomposing your organic matter need a steady supply of oxygen to function at maximum potential, as Chapter 3 describes. Also, mixing organic materials on the outside of a pile into the inside so that everything decomposes evenly is a good practice. Tumbling composters are designed to do precisely that: You rotate or tumble them to facilitate the incorporation of oxygen and the mixing of ingredients without swinging a pitchfork or poking the pile with an aerating tool.

A basic tumbler style is shaped like a canister that you roll around the yard. Other styles include a large drum that rests on its aboveground stand with a hand crank to turn it, and smaller units that you grasp and spin as they rest on slightly concave pads on the ground.

One problem I've experienced with tumblers is that fresh, moist materials occasionally clump into a compacted heavy ball within the first few days of rotating. The big blob of organic matter loses out on the benefits of aeration offered by tumbling. Figure 5-1 illustrates a tumbler style that contains a metal rod running through its center. As the materials tumble within, they fall and break against the rod, which helps to prevent clods from forming. Of course, if you have another tumbler style, you may break up any clods that form with a tool or your gloved hands.

Figure 5-1: A tumbling compost container.

An oft-touted advantage of tumblers is that they make it easy to turn compost. In theory this is true, but in practice, an oversize tumbler fully loaded with moist organic matter is not lightweight and requires some strength to rotate. A properly moistened composting effort starts out with 40 to 60 percent water by weight. How easily you can turn the unit depends upon its style and weight, how much and what type of organic matter it's filled with (fresh moist manure weighs more than dry straw, for example), and any physical limitations you may have. If you like the notion of a tumbler but harbor any physical concerns, find fellow composters in your area who will let you take their tumblers out for a spin. Ask local garden clubs. Some gardens open to the public also open up their composting areas. Don't be shy. I've never met a composter who didn't enjoy sharing stories about their composting experiences.

You may also consider a smaller tumbling unit that's easier to rotate. However, composting is most efficient (giving you finished compost faster) when the bulk of organic matter starts out at least 1 cubic yard (1 cubic meter) in size (3 feet tall by 3 feet wide by 3 feet deep, or 1 meter each way). If your container is considerably smaller, the process will take longer. Of course, this is true of any container style, not just tumblers. The importance of container size is discussed further in the sidebar "Testing a tumbler."

Finally, a tumbler's enclosed sides foil pests from rooting through the organic matter for kitchen scraps. If the tumbler sits on the ground, ensure that its access panels fasten securely. (Some critters are mighty clever at opening things.) Tumblers that rest on aboveground stands are even more pest-proof, but they also require tight-fitting doors.

Testing a tumbler

A disadvantage to some tumblers (as well as non-tumbling containers) is that their size doesn't hold sufficient organic matter for fast and efficient composting. I saw this firsthand when trying different styles at my county cooperative extension demonstration site. What started out as less than 1 cubic yard (1 cubic meter) of material (the minimum size for efficient decomposition) shrunk in half within days. This is good and bad. You want the material to get smaller in volume as it decomposes, but now the overall bulk is much smaller than the ideal size to self-insulate and maintain heat. Tumbling (adding air) cools the temperature of the organic matter for a short time until the decomposers rev up again. But with limited material, the pile doesn't have sufficient mass to reheat up to high temps. We monitored temperatures and moisture, adjusted the content and ratio of materials, and poked, prodded and peered into the depths to fine-tune the process. Ultimately, we determined that our fine-tuning took more time than the plain square open bin that was turned a couple times with a pitchfork and left alone. It always produced more compost, faster than the tumblers. I'm not saying these units won't work for you, just that they aren't magical. Someone still needs to manage the show!

Bins of all types

I define "bin" pretty broadly for this discussion. Just about any container that isn't a tumbler falls into the bin category. Following are characteristics to consider.

Open or closed

Open bins are just that: Some combination of their top, sides, and bottom are open to the air, precipitation, and pests. Examples include homemade square bins made of shipping pallets and manufactured circular enclosures made of lightweight recycled plastic with pre-formed ventilation holes, such as the Presto GEOBIN (check it out at www.prestoproducts.com/consumer/garden/bins.htm). Open bins have a number of advantages:

- ✔ They're easier and less expensive to erect, with fewer construction materials required.
- ✔ Adding more compostables over time is easy.
- ✔ Stirring up the mix with an aerating tool is easy.
- ✔ Open ground beneath the bin allows soil organisms to gain quick access, speeding decomposition.
- ✔ Open sides and/or an open top take advantage of free air and water (and snow).

But they also have some disadvantages:

- ✔ Open sides and/or an open top allow material to dry out faster or become too wet, depending on climate.
- ✔ Pests have easy access.
- ✔ The appearance of organic matter may be unsightly.

Closed bins are sealed from the elements. Homemade wooden bins with hinged tops and sheet metal bottoms (with drainage holes) serve as an example. Many manufactured options are available, such as tumblers (see the earlier section "Taking a turn with tumblers") or square plastic bins, similar to the one shown in Figure 5-2.

Figure 5-2: A plastic, closed compost container.

Like open bins, closed ones have some advantages. Closed bins

- ✔ Hide organic matter for a tidier appearance
- ✔ Retain moisture and heat more evenly
- ✔ Inhibit pest access (see "Keeping Wildlife Out of Your Container" later in the chapter)

Following are the downsides to closed bins:

- ✔ They require more materials, making them potentially more expensive.
- ✔ Adding and accessing organic materials is more difficult.
- ✔ They're often smaller in size, thus holding less organic material.

Stationary versus movable

Stationery bins sit in one place for the duration, unless you exert time and effort to relocate them. Examples include a bin made of concrete blocks or a wooden three-bin unit (see Chapter 6).

Movable composters are free to "get up and move around the cabin." Or, more accurately, you're free to move them around your yard with little effort. This is a nice feature if you have just one container and want to turn your compost regularly to aerate or remoisten it. Lift the container off the pile, set it aside, and fork or shovel the organic matter back in. Examples of easy-to-move containers include a homemade wire enclosure, a lightweight plastic model without a bottom, and a manufactured wire bin with collapsible sides, as shown in Figure 5-3.

Figure 5-3: A wire compost bin with collapsible sides.

Multi-bin systems

Just one square bin can hold and produce a significant amount of organic matter, and an advantage of a basic square shape is that you can quickly add second or third adjacent bins to meet changing needs for more composting space. (Or you can remove a bin if you need less space.) If you answer "yes" to any or all of the following questions, you may feel most comfortable starting with just one square bin:

- ✔ Are you new to composting?
- ✔ Are you unsure how much organic material your yard and household will generate?
- ✔ Are you unsure how much time and effort you want to put into composting?

As you gain experience, you can easily add adjacent second and third bins. You may eventually reach the composting output of a friend of mine who used six bins in a row at a community garden! By the time organic matter reached the last bin, it was dark, rich compost, ready to incorporate into the garden.

Following are a few more questions to consider:

✔ Do you plan to maintain compost piles throughout the year, adding new materials as they become available?

✔ Does your yard and household generate a considerable amount of organic matter that you want to recycle?

✔ Do you want to generate a lot of finished compost?

✔ Do you enjoy turning organic materials by hand?

If you answered "yes" to any or all of those questions, you're a prime candidate for a three-bin compost system. Three squarish bins share common sidewalls. This style uses space efficiently and makes it convenient to turn organic material from one bin into the next. Basically, you fill Bin #1 with organic matter and start it cooking. When it's partially decomposed and ready to turn, you shift it into Bin #2 and start a new pile of fresh organic matter in Bin #1. When Bin #2 decomposes further, you turn it into Bin #3 to finish decomposing. And so the cycle continues. (Chapter 8 offers complete instructions for using three bins efficiently.)

Of course, you can always just split the difference with a two-bin system, rotating organic matter back and forth.

Kitchen composters

Not all products sold as kitchen composters create useable compost from your kitchen waste. Some are simply attractive holding units that blend unobtrusively with your kitchen décor until you have time to dump the organic matter into your outdoor bin. Others, such as bokashi composters, start the decomposition ball rolling, but you must eventually transfer the organic matter outdoors, either to a compost pile or to a hole in the ground where it continues to decompose into substances that improve soil and provide nutrients to plants. (See Chapter 4 for details on trench composting.)

An outdoor option for composting kitchen waste is an underground "food digester," such as the Green Cone designed to deter pests.

But what do you do with kitchen scraps if you live in an apartment or condo with zero access to outdoor space for composting? Consider harboring a bin of worms to chow down on your food waste. Called *vermicomposting,* this method is fascinating and effective. Worms consume at least half their weight in food per day. So, if you have a pound of worms, they'll process about a half pound of scraps. Chapter 10 provides the complete rundown on how to set up a squirm of worms.

If worms aren't your thing, another indoor option that produces finished compost is an electric-powered unit that mixes and aerates just about all kitchen scraps, including meats, fish, and dairy. Finished compost drops into a holding tray where it continues to cure and you can access it when convenient.

I describe all these options (except the worms) for composting kitchen waste in more detail in the following sections.

Countertop crocks

You may find it convenient to stockpile kitchen scraps destined for your outdoor bin in a small countertop container within handy reach of food prep areas. Resembling miniature garbage cans or ice buckets, these units hold about a gallon's worth of scraps (that's about 3.8 liters).

Look for crocks that feature tight-fitting lids and activated charcoal filters within the lid to keep odors in check. Bad smells or fly invasions shouldn't occur if you empty the container regularly — every couple days or at least weekly, depending on what you're filling it with and the temperature in your house. Filters last about three months. Factor in the cost of replacement filters when making your purchase decision.

You don't have to buy a special product to stockpile kitchen scraps. Toss them into a plastic food storage container with a tight lid and store it in the freezer to forestall any odors and flies. Transfer it to your outdoor compost operation when convenient. Rinse the container outdoors and pour the water on the compost pile contents.

Rub lemon juice, vinegar, or baking soda inside kitchen scrap collection containers to remove odors naturally.

Bokashi composting

Bokashi is a Japanese term referring to a process of fermenting organic matter. Bokashi kitchen composting mixes scraps with an inoculant (called bokashi) of beneficial microorganisms that hasten fermentation anaerobically (without oxygen), while avoiding the offensive odors typical of anaerobic decomposition. (Read more about anaerobic composting in Chapter 4.) Bokashi inoculant is usually sold as dry wheat or rice bran embedded with microorganisms and their food source, such as molasses.

Bokashi containers don't create useable compost. The closed system ferments (pickles) kitchen scraps, starting the breakdown of organic matter. At the end of the fermenting period, food scraps are still recognizable because they're pickled, not decomposed. Final decomposition takes place outdoors after you bury the material in the soil or a compost bin. Consider the following advantages and disadvantages to decide whether a bokashi system is right for you.

Here are the pros of utilizing a bokashi system:

- ✔ The initial indoor fermentation period makes food waste less of a draw for pests after transferring it outdoors.

- ✔ Soil microbes quickly break down remaining organic matter after the material is placed outdoors.

- ✔ Food wastes that must be kept out of traditional, open-to-the-air (aerobic) compost bins, such as meat and dairy, can be put in a bokashi container.

- ✔ The container commands only a small amount of indoor space.

- ✔ Liquid drained off during the fermentation period can be highly diluted and used as a plant food.

Of course, the bokashi system has its downsides, too. These include the following:

- ✔ Purchasing bokashi is an ongoing expense.

- ✔ Scraps must be chopped into small pieces.

- ✔ Rotten or moldy scraps should not be composted.

- ✔ Material must be buried outdoors at least 8 to 12 inches deep in the soil or compost pile after initial fermentation.

- ✔ Two or more containers are needed to continue processing scraps while the first container ferments.

Bokashi composting requires an airtight container, with an optional spout at the base for draining liquid created during fermentation. (Dispose of liquid or dilute one part liquid with 100 parts water and use it to fertilize plants.) You can buy containers or make your own from a five-gallon bucket with a tight lid.

Enter "bokashi composting" into your favorite Internet search engine to explore the method, including finding bokashi inoculant and instructions for creating and using a bokashi container.

Green Cone

The Green Cone composter is sometimes described as an in-ground food digester. It can handle all sorts of kitchen waste and food scraps, including meats, fish, bones, dairy, and oils. However, if you're going to add those items, secure the unit from pests (see the tip later in this section).

The Green Cone has four parts: an underground basket, two aboveground cones, and a lid. Bury the bottom, and all those wonderful soil organisms described in Chapter 3 can climb right in and get to work breaking down your scraps. Aboveground, the Green Cone looks like, well, a green cone. Within it is a second, smaller cone that fits securely over the bottom portion to inhibit pests. You pop your kitchen scraps in the top cone, which has a lid.

The Green Cone wasn't designed to produce useable finished compost. It's intended to recycle food scraps and keep them out of the waste stream. Most materials will break down into carbon dioxide and liquids that spread into the surrounding soil. Alternatively, you can harvest residue that remains in the basket after 9 to 12 months and add it to a compost pile or bury it in your garden.

The primary advantages of the Green Cone are that it

- ✔ Keeps all kitchen scraps out of the waste stream.

- ✔ Doesn't need turning or mixing.

- ✔ Requires limited outdoor space to set up.

The main disadvantages of the Green Cone are that it

- ✔ Doesn't produce much useable compost.

- ✔ Needs excellent soil drainage and a sunny location to work at peak efficiency.

- ✔ May attract digging pests.

- ✔ May fill with organic material faster than decomposition occurs. If the cone becomes ¼ to ⅓ full, organic matter (which may be wet and stinky) needs to be removed and buried in the garden or other compost pile. Operating two units simultaneously reduces this problem. One can be left to decompose while the other is filled with fresh scraps.

 To forestall pests digging around or into your Green Cone, wrap the underground basket in tight wire mesh, such as hardware cloth, before burying it. After installing the unit, firmly compact the surrounding soil and cover it with bricks, rocks, or pavers to discourage animals that are drawn to freshly dug soil. If pests are a problem, limit attractive ingredients, such as meat, fish, and dairy.

You can find out more about the Green Cone system, including where to purchase one, online at www.greencone.com.

NatureMill

This automatic, electric-powered unit includes an upper chamber that holds food scraps and a lower chamber for finished compost. A heater keeps the upper chamber's contents warm to facilitate decomposition. A fan pulls air in, and it exits via an air filter to control odor. The unit's computer chip tells the motor when to operate the upper chamber's mixing bar, which rotates for several minutes at a time (that's the mesmerizing stage). When organic matter has decomposed sufficiently, the unit sends it through a trap door into a holding tray in the bottom chamber. There, it sits to "cure" further until you're ready to harvest it. In the meantime, you refill the upper chamber with more scraps.

The most enticing features of the NatureMill composter are that it

- ✔ Composts typical kitchen scraps as well as meat, fish, dairy, and oils
- ✔ Accommodates up to 4 pounds per day, so you can add scraps as frequently as you want
- ✔ Works fast to turn scraps into compost
- ✔ Operates indoors or outdoors (with electric plug)
- ✔ Features a compact size — 20 inches high x 20 inches long x 12 inches wide (50.8 x 50.8 x 30.5 centimeters, respectively)

Following are a few disadvantages of the system:

- ✔ The motor that turns the mixing bar is noisier than the unit's ongoing low hum.
- ✔ Scraps need to be chopped into 4-inch pieces.
- ✔ The unit is more expensive than some other options.

You can find out more about the NatureMill system, including purchasing information, online at www.naturemill.com.

Keeping Wildlife Out of Your Container

Depending on where you live, creatures attracted to a compost pile may include rodents, cats, dogs, foxes, raccoons, coyotes, badgers, and javelina. In some regions, even bears may appear in backyards as development spreads into their ranges and normal food supplies become scarce.

People are the ones usually encroaching on the animals' territory — don't blame them for seeking food.

When wild creatures tangle with humans, the animals are usually the losers, so it's better to deter them from the get-go rather than try to change their routine once they've discovered there's a regular food supply in your backyard. You can do this by eliminating specific ingredients from your compost and by using bins with characteristics that prevent animal access (or at least make it more difficult).

Eliminating enticing ingredients

Don't put meat, fish, bones, dairy products, grease, or oil in your compost bin. This simple step reduces the likelihood of midnight prowlers rooting through your pile. Avoid using blood meal as a nitrogen source or accelerator to speed up the composting process (you can find more on accelerators in Chapter 8). Its scent, though not particularly noticeable to humans, may attract unwanted critters to the pile, including your family dog. Cover kitchen scraps or vegetable garden trimmings with an 8-inch layer of dry brown materials, such as leaves, straw, or organic matter that's in the process of decomposing. Using two or three side-by-side bins makes this easy. Pitchfork or shovel material stockpiled in one bin onto the freshly added scraps in a second bin.

Using bin characteristics to exclude creatures

Manufacturers of compost bins know that animals can be pretty smart when it comes to gaining access to the contents of your bin, so they design their bins with specific features that help keep animals out. The following bin styles and features inhibit unwanted access:

- ✔ Fully enclosed bins (including solid bottoms) with securely latched lids

- ✔ Tumblers resting on aboveground supports

- ✔ Small aeration holes or holes covered with wire mesh

- ✔ Bin styles designed to deter pests such as the Green Cone (refer to the earlier section)

When building your own bins or modifying less secure manufactured bins, these ideas may help you prevent pests from gaining access:

✔ Cover aeration holes with hardware cloth or wire mesh to prevent rodents from squeezing through. (Rodents chew plastic mesh.)

✔ Build wood bins with tight mesh wire sides and hinged, fiberglass or wood lids.

✔ Place heavy covers (such as wood shipping palettes) on the top of large open bins to block easy access.

✔ Set bricks on top of easy-to-remove lids.

Bugs, ants, and flies, oh my!

Insects are an essential component of a healthy compost pile, so don't sweat their presence. Read more about who's doing what in the compost pile in Chapter 3. If you follow the steps in Chapters 7 and 8 for constructing and maintaining your pile, the likelihood of harboring hosts of undesirable pest insects is slim.

Bugs

When did humans become so "bug-averse?" In fact, critters of all sorts that inhabit the pile don't do much harm and can provide you with quite a sideshow. When I turn compost, lizards scurry closer along the block wall to get a look at juicy offerings that my pitchfork may have uncovered. I don't even have to stand still; a bold lizard will dash in, grab its take-out meal, and head home with dinner hanging from its mouth. If I turn my back for a minute, birds also hop about the pile, snapping up juicy white grubs unearthed in finished compost. Be on the lookout to see what intriguing native creatures may be feasting on insects from your compost heap.

Ants

Unlike flies that set course for a wet pile, ants like dry living quarters. Moistening and turning the pile frequently can send them packing. Some regular ants always seem to be scurrying through a compost pile, and they aren't a reason for concern. However, if you have nasty biting ants, get them under control as soon as possible so they don't spread colonies to other areas of your landscape. For a natural pesticide treatment, try one of the following:

✔ **Spinosad:** This is a pesticide derived from a naturally occurring soil bacterium. If you're an organic gardener, look for a product that states on its container that spinosad is the active ingredient and that it's certified for use in organic gardens.

✓ **Orange peel slurry:** To make a slurry, grind orange peels with water in a blender. Flood the ant mound with the slurry immediately after making it so it doesn't lose its effectiveness.

✓ **Boiling water:** Pouring boiling water in the mound is another option.

✓ **Aromatic plant:** The pungent yet pleasant smell of a particular mint species *(Mentha requienii)* deters ants. You may find it for sale as Corsican mint in the United States or pennyroyal mint in the United Kingdom.

Flies

If you find yourself with the problem of annoying insects, you're most likely dealing with household flies. Flies are drawn to moist, rotting organic matter on which they lay their eggs. Hatching fly larvae (better known by the unpleasant-sounding moniker *maggots*) remain in the pile three to five days, guzzling down organic matter before pupating and emerging as adult flies to repeat the cycle.

If you have troublesome numbers of flies buzzing around, your pile needs attention. Assess your pile's conditions and ingredients to determine whether you need to implement one of these corrective measures:

✓ Turn the pile. This introduces oxygen to dry out overly wet material and/or heat up the pile. (Fly larvae die in high temperatures.) Make sure materials on the outer edges get worked into the center so that everything has a chance to "feel the heat."

✓ Add more green nitrogen materials, such as grass clippings or manure, to boost heat levels.

✓ Add more dry carbon materials (such as leaves or straw) to counteract an abundance of overly wet nitrogen materials (like manure, grass clippings, and coffee grounds).

✓ Always bury food scraps within the center of the pile or cover fresh additions with an 8-inch (20-centimeter) layer of dry leaves or straw.

Shopping for a Composter: A Buyer's Guide

The most common frustration I hear from gardeners about composting in manufactured bins sounds something like this: "It takes longer than I thought it would to produce finished compost." Unfortunately, compost containers (despite some of the marketing materials that accompany them) aren't magical devices whereby you drop in straw, wave your wand-like compost thermometer, and presto — out spills black gold! The basic needs of decomposer organisms must still be met, including an appropriate mix of carbon and nitrogen materials chopped into small pieces, moisture and aeration during the process, and sufficient mass to build up and retain temperature levels. Your efforts in meeting these requirements favor the types of mesophilic and thermophilic organisms that do the bulk of the work. You can read all about them in Chapter 3.

Whether tumblers or bins, containers have common characteristics as described in the following list. Considering these options sets you on the right path to choosing the container that's best for your situation:

- ✔ **Size:** When comparison shopping, keep in mind that a container's size is often the limiting factor in its ability to produce compost quickly. If the container holds less than 1 cubic yard (1 cubic meter) of materials (the minimum size for efficient decomposition), you can still work with it. But you need to manage the contents, air, moisture, and temperature more regularly if you want speedy compost, just as you would with a freestanding pile or homemade bin. If you're in no hurry and just want a tidy receptacle to contain a relatively small amount of organic leftovers, then container size is not as important a factor. Of course, don't forget that a big container typically weighs more as well!

- ✔ **Weight:** If it's a tumbler, you want to be able to easily rotate it when it's full of heavy, wet organic matter. If it's not a tumbler, and you use just one container, it's nice to be able to lift it up and off the organic matter to set it aside for turning or reloading.

- ✔ **Height:** Make sure you can easily lift your pitchfork or shovel loaded with organic materials into the container. It's typically less fatiguing to rest your pitchfork or shovel on the side of the container as you empty it, rather than to hoist it upwards above shoulder level.

- ✔ **Assembly required:** Most bins require some assembly. Connectors such as screws or bolts usually hold up longer than plastic tabs that crack or break after a season or two in extreme weather. Look for sturdy, rigid construction at joints. Loose connections can come apart and cause the container to collapse when you're poking around in the midst of the bin with a tool to aerate organic matter.

- ✔ **Lids:** Look for sufficiently large top openings to add fresh organic matter. Will your loaded-up pitchfork or shovel fit with room to spare? Or do you need to use your hands to stuff materials in? Perhaps you'd like a smaller access door within the lid that you can flip open to toss in the day's kitchen scraps without removing the entire lid.

✔ **Pest deterrents:** Lids should tighten securely to protect against enterprising pests and strong winds. At the same time, you want to be able to lift lids to add more organic matter without a lot of fuss. Containers should be fully enclosed, including a solid or tight wire-mesh bottom. Some open-to-the-ground containers have optional bottoms that you can buy. Containers lifted on stands above ground level are also good pest deterrents, but they still need secure lids to foil climbers.

Check with your regional parks department, game and fish, wildlife, or other natural resource management agencies for information on local pest problems and recommended deterrents.

✔ **Access panels:** Some units offer sliding trap doors at the bottom to provide access to the finished compost. Check the dimensions to see whether your spade will fit inside. Otherwise, you'll need to scoop compost out by hand or use a hand trowel. Some units have panels on multiple sides. If the composter has no bottom, lifting it up and setting it aside to get at your finished product is often easier than poking around in small portholes.

✔ **Aeration and drainage holes:** Air and water are important ingredients in composting. If bins are fully enclosed, there must be some method for allowing air in and moisture out. Without drainage, the contents of the container turn wet and stinky and the decomposition process slows.

Chapter 6

Erecting Your Own Compost Containers

*W*hen it comes to compost bin construction, you can get by just fine with a simple and inexpensive bin you build yourself. After all, composting occurs when organic matter is piled in a heap and left to rot (as I describe in Chapter 4), so obviously the decomposer organisms don't care if a high-rise condo surrounds their food supply. However, after getting a primer on composting containers in Chapter 5, you may have decided to organize your composting area with some type of structure.

Before you head out to buy a manufactured bin, I suggest getting your feet wet with one or more of the basic bin styles I describe in this chapter. You'll learn just as much about the composting process with these options, and your experiences may highlight useful features in a manufactured bin. (On the other hand, you may discover that your homemade bin suits you perfectly, and you can use the money you would have spent on a bin to purchase more plants for your garden!)

With the exception of the wood and wire three-bin system, all the bins I describe in this chapter are easy to make, as you can see from the step-by-step instructions. I know they're easy, because I've tried them all over the years, and I don't consider myself very handy in the tool or carpentry departments!

Some bin construction progresses more smoothly with an extra set of hands or physical strength, and I note instances where this is the case, along with the advantages and disadvantages of each style, a materials list, and step-by-step instructions.

Transforming Recycled Items into Inexpensive Containers

Because composting is all about recycling organic matter, it seems appropriate for composting bins to be made from recycled materials as well. The two bin options I describe in this section warm recyclers' hearts. You're likely to obtain them at no cost — or dirt-cheap.

Wood shipping pallets

Wood shipping pallets are used as platforms to support consumer goods being transported by forklifts and other equipment. Recycled pallets are my favorite option for creating easy-to-build and highly effective composting systems, especially when you have a lot of organic matter to process.

Every composting container has its advantages and disadvantages, and converted pallets are no exception. Following are a few of the pros and cons:

✔ **Advantages**

- **Cost:** They're free! You've probably seen pallets piled at construction sites or stacked at loading docks behind businesses and warehouses, awaiting recycling or disposal. Explain to the head honcho you'd like to recycle some to make a compost bin. Most places pay to have them hauled away and are happy to oblige. Look pallets over to make sure they're in decent shape before carting them home.

- **Size:** Pallets are presized to perfection. No measuring, no cutting, no hammering. Pallet sizes vary considerably based upon country, industry standards, and the type of goods being transported, but to simplify, in North America, pallets commonly measure 40 x 48 inches, which creates a bin size that is ideal for composting. A comparable European Union pallet size for effective composting is 1,000 x 1,200 millimeters. Don't feel obligated to find these exact sizes. Many other options work, as long as they provide you with a 3- to 6-foot (1- to 2-meter) square shape.

✔ **Disadvantages**

- **Weight:** Depending on size and type of wood, a single pallet can weigh 20 to 50 pounds (9 to 23 kilograms). Heft it and see whether you can comfortably move it around. If not, keep searching for others.

- **Portability:** Pallets aren't as easy to reposition around the yard as some choices, but they're still faster to move and set up than concrete blocks or straw bales.

- **Openness to pests:** See Chapter 5 for ideas on inhibiting pests.

Materials

All you need to gather for this project are pallets, ties, and a tool to cut the ties, and you're ready to get started. Here are the specifics:

✔ Four same-sized pallets per bin. Pallets with narrow spaces between slats hold back organic materials better than those with wide spaces.

✔ Baling wire or nylon rope to lash pallets together at the corners.

✔ Wire cutters or a utility knife to cut ties.

Instructions

One person can assemble a shipping pallet compost bin, although it goes smoother with two: one to hold the pallets upright and steady while the other ties them together. Follow these steps to erect the bin shown in Figure 6-1:

1. **Level the ground where your bin will be.**

2. **Set the pallets upright in a box shape.**

3. **Lash the pallets securely together at the corners with wire or rope ties.**

   The front pallet acts as a hinged door, allowing you to access your compost by undoing the ties on one side and swinging it open. You can also remove the entire pallet to have wider access when adding or turning organic matter.

 Add second and third bins to your first shipping pallet bin using common side walls. You need three pallets for each additional bin.

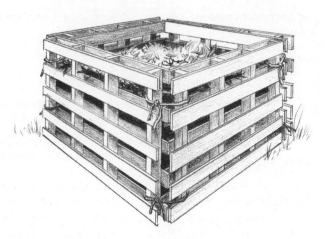

Figure 6-1: Shipping pallet compost bin.

Recycled garbage can

Another inexpensive recycling option for a compost container is a large, recycled garbage can. Contact the department responsible for trash pickup (it may be called solid waste disposal) in your area, whether it be a town, city, county, or other office. Many communities recycle their no-longer-useable garbage cans as compost containers to residents, either free or for a nominal fee. You may want to gather a group of neighbors (including someone with a truck) to pick up several at once.

Check with these same municipal departments (or the Council departments in the United Kingdom) to see whether they offer reduced prices on manufactured compost containers. Some may offer promotions (even free manufactured containers) to encourage community involvement in composting, recycling, and waste reduction.

Garbage can styles vary, of course. Some come with secure lids, which is great if you want to keep pests out. Most agencies have already removed any wheels on the can. Some may remove the bottom of the trash can and/or punch aeration holes. If you have a preference for bottom/no bottom or holes/no holes, ask in advance to see whether your request can be accommodated.

Using recycled garbage cans as composting bins has upsides and downsides:

✔ **Advantages**

- **Cost:** They're free or inexpensive.

- **Portability:** They're easy to move to different areas in the garden.

- **Protection from pests:** Cans with lids keep pests at bay.

✔ **Disadvantages**

- **Size and shape:** Most garbage cans aren't quite large enough to contain the optimal amount of organic matter (1 cubic yard or 1 cubic meter) needed to self-insulate and promote fast decomposition.

- **Appearance:** With apologies to Gertrude Stein, a garbage can is a garbage can is a garbage can. Let your kids loose on it with some paints and brushes to dress it up a bit, or hide the can in the back corner of your landscape!

Materials

The great thing about this compost bin project is that it requires so little — a recycled garbage receptacle obtained from your municipality. If this isn't an option where you live, you may check with neighbors or put an advertisement in your local paper or on Web sites asking to recycle a can someone is tossing.

Instructions

Not surprisingly, lifting or moving the bin into position is the most challenging part of erecting a recycled garbage can compost bin. You just set your can in place and start filling it up (see Chapter 8 for compost ingredients). Wasn't that easy?

Building Bins with Wire, Bales, or Wood

If recycled shipping pallets or garbage containers aren't available to you, this section covers a variety of other options for you to construct. Some of them may cost you nothing if you're able to repurpose or scrounge the supplies. Others require a more substantial investment but pay off in the end.

Positioning your garbage can to the best advantage

If your can comes with a lid but no bottom and you want to keep pests at bay, dig a hole about 1 foot (0.3 meters) deep and "sink" the base of the container into the soil.

If your can has no lid, no bottom, and is wider at the top, tapering towards the bottom, the narrowing shape makes it somewhat more difficult to aerate the organic matter at the bottom when stirring with a compost fork or aeration tool. Setting the can upside down so the wider section becomes the base alleviates this issue. When it's time to turn the material, lift it up, set it aside, and fork the materials back into it. When choosing a site for your composting, allow sufficient space to set the can to the side, and you'll save labor in the long run.

Hardware cloth circular wire bin

When you only have enough space for one bin to corral and turn your compost, my personal favorite is a simple, circular enclosure made of mesh wire hardware cloth. When compost is ready to be turned, lift the lightweight wire bin, set it to the side of the pile, and fork the organic matter back in for another round of decomposition. Select an original site that gives you enough space nearby to reset the bin when you're ready to turn the contents.

Wire bins are excellent, quick-to-construct holding units if you score a windfall of leaves, straw, or other dry carbon materials that need stockpiling until you're ready to add them to your compost. This is also the perfect container for making leaf mold, a type of compost with leaves as the sole ingredient (see Chapter 7).

Hardware cloth isn't cloth at all, but stiff galvanized mesh screen. It maintains its shape better over the long term than poultry wire (also called chicken wire), which has a tendency to get bent or crushed without support poles. Hardware cloth bins stand firmly upright without supports. Otherwise, the advantages and disadvantages of bins made of hardware cloth or poultry wire are the same and are listed here:

✔ **Advantages**

- **Cost:** They're inexpensive, or even free if you have wire from other projects to recycle.

- **Size:** They're good for small spaces.

- **Ease of use:** They're easy to assemble, disassemble, and store (tightly rolled).

- **Weight/portability:** They're lightweight and easy to move. Just pick up the empty wire circle and carry it to a new location in the landscape.

- **Air circulation:** They provide good aeration for rainy climates.

✔ **Disadvantages**

- **Openness to pests:** See Chapter 5 for ideas on inhibiting pests.

- **Dryness:** Organic matter dries out rapidly. Obviously this is the opposite of the previously mentioned advantageous aeration! Especially in arid climates or windy weather, compost in open wire bins dries out faster than compost contained by more solid enclosures.

You can alleviate dryness by throwing a tarp over the entire bin or by remoistening the organic material regularly. You can also wrap the exterior sides with burlap or heavy, corrugated cardboard. As the cardboard starts to disintegrate, rip it up and toss it in the compost. Rewrap the enclosure with fresh cardboard. Shops and businesses always seem to have a plentiful supply of cardboard to recycle.

Materials

Here's yet another bin style that requires just a few simple materials to complete your project:

✔ 10- to 12½-foot (3- to 4-meter) length of 36-inch-wide (1-meter-wide) hardware cloth. (Divide your total wire length by 3.14 to obtain the bin's potential diameter.)

✔ Baling wire to use as ties.

✔ Wire cutters.

✔ Metal file.

✔ *Optional:* Pliers.

This size wire forms a bin about 3 to 3.5 feet (1 meter) in diameter and 3 feet (1 meter) high, holding about 1 cubic yard (1 cubic meter) of organic matter, a perfect amount for a pile to self-insulate and heat for faster decomposition (Chapter 8 discusses optimal pile sizes). This bin height is easy to shovel or fork materials over, as well as to reach into with a tool to aerate the contents.

Hardware cloth and poultry wire are sold in rolls of various lengths and widths. If you plan to make only one bin, you may be able to buy a roll that is close to your desired bin size and skip the step of cutting wire. If you have leftovers from a roll of hardware cloth, scraps make excellent compost screens. Chapter 10 explains how to make and use a compost screen.

Instructions

This section walks you through the steps of creating the bin shown in Figure 6-2.

Wire that has been tightly rolled has a hidden desire to spring loose from the shape you're trying to form, so an extra set of hands can be helpful to hold it while you tie the ends together.

1. **Use wire cutters to cut the hardware cloth to the desired length.**

   Cut flush with the cross-wires to eliminate sharp points that can scratch unprotected hands and arms when working with the bin.

2. **Use a steel file to lightly smooth any rough edges that remain after cutting.**

3. **Form the length of wire into a cylinder.**

4. **Secure the ends of the wire cylinder together with wire ties.**

   If the wire is stiff, using pliers to twist the wire ties securely is easier than using your fingers to twist them.

5. **Set the wire enclosure up in your compost area.**

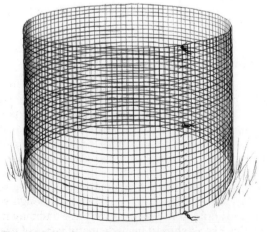

Figure 6-2: Hardware cloth wire compost bin.

Poultry wire circular bin

You may know poultry wire by its other name, chicken wire. Whatever you call it, it makes a decent circular composting bin as long as you include support posts in your construction. Because you need to pound posts into the ground to support your poultry wire bin, you should test the ground first. If it's too hard or rocky to pound stakes into, scout another location or consider a different bin design, such as the support-less hardware cloth bin in the preceding section. You can also water the ground in advance, allowing the water to seep in slowly for a day or two until the ground is soft enough to pound the posts several inches deep.

The pros and cons of poultry wire circular bins are the same as those for hardware cloth circular bins; you can find that information in the preceding section.

Materials

Posts are needed to support this flexible wire bin, but otherwise the materials list is similar to that of the preceding project. You need the following:

- ✔ 10- to 12½-foot (3- to 4-meter) length of 36-inch-wide (1-meter-wide) poultry wire (also called chicken wire) or a similar material made from plastic, called plastic netting.

  If you garden in critter-dense country, note that animals can chomp through plastic netting.

- ✔ Baling wire to use as ties.

- ✔ Wire cutters.

- ✔ Two or three 4- to 6-foot-tall (1- to 2-meter-tall) support posts.

- ✔ Hammer or mallet.

- ✔ *Optional:* Pliers.

The following post materials are readily available at home improvement and hardware stores. You may also find useable lengths at non-profit stores that stock donated home improvement goods to keep them out of the waste stream, such as Habitat for Humanity's ReStores. (You can find a listing of ReStores in the United States and Canada at www.habitat.org/env/restores.aspx.)

- ✔ **PVC pipe:** Typically used for plumbing and irrigation, PVC (polyvinyl chloride) lasts 15 to 20 years, although when exposed to sunlight it discolors with age and may become brittle. Even so, it should provide many years of use for your compost bin.

✔ **Rebar:** Metal concrete reinforcing bar, commonly called *rebar,* rusts quickly but lasts indefinitely. If you don't like rebar's rusty appearance, coat it with a rust-preventing paint.

✔ **Metal fence posts:** Galvanized metal fence posts have pointed tips that facilitate pounding into difficult soil.

✔ **Wooden stakes:** If you have wooden stakes on hand, go ahead and use them. But because wood doesn't hold up as long in the elements as the other materials listed, if you need to buy something, I suggest you opt for durability over the long haul.

Instructions

Wire that has been tightly rolled has a hidden desire to spring loose from the shape you're trying to form, so an extra set of hands can be helpful to hold it while you tie the ends together.

Follow these steps to create a circular compost bin made of poultry wire or plastic netting and support posts:

1. **Use wire cutters to cut the poultry wire or plastic netting to the desired length.**

   Cutting poultry wire to the appropriate length leaves behind sharp ends, but because this wire is flexible (unlike hardware cloth), you can fold the entire cut side back several inches, creating a straight, "smooth" edge.

2. **Form the length of wire into a cylinder.**

3. **Secure the ends of the wire cylinder together with wire ties.**

   If the wire is heavy and stiff, using pliers to twist the wire ties is easier than using your fingers.

4. **Set the wire enclosure up in your compost area.**

5. **Space two or three posts evenly around the inside of the bin. Hold the posts tightly against the wire and pound them into the ground with a hammer or mallet.**

Straw-bale bin

Straw bales can be stacked in any size and configuration to create a simple and relatively inexpensive bin. As an organic material, straw breaks down and decomposes over time, and you can eventually incorporate it into your compost pile as a carbon ingredient. (Chapter 7 covers details about straw and other composting ingredients.) Straw is a convenient choice if you're just getting into composting and aren't sure what type of bin you want. You'll gain experience without paying for a bin or materials that may not suit your situation.

How many bales to use depends on the size of individual bales available in your area, how high you plan to stack them, and how much square footage you want for composting. Bales stacked in two or three layers provide sufficient area for composting, although you could get away with just one layer if lifting the bales is a challenge.

If you want to turn compost regularly, stack straw bales to form three sides of a square or rectangular shape, leaving the fourth side open for access. You can also form an enclosed square, filling it full of materials to decompose on their own time schedule without turning. If you get the urge to turn, you can always pull out a couple bales to create access.

Here are the pros and cons of building a compost bin using straw bales:

✔ **Advantages**

- **Speed:** This type of bin is quick to build.

- **Adaptability:** It's easy to expand (or shrink) your bin's size and add adjacent bins.

- **Insulation:** Bales provide good insulation to maintain moisture and heat within the compost.

✔ **Disadvantages**

- **Weight:** Bales are heavy to transport and lift. If you can't comfortably tote 50 to 80 pounds (23 to 36 kilograms), straw bales aren't the best option!

- **Unavailability:** Bales may not be readily available, depending on where you live.

- **Openness to pests:** See Chapter 5 for ideas on inhibiting pests.

- **Breakdown:** Bales aren't permanent, and as straw breaks down, it loses its tidy appearance. Stacks may lose their stability, sag, and look unkempt.

Materials

To create a straw bale composting bin, the only materials you need are five or six two-string straw bales. Based on the number of wire or twine lengths holding it together, a straw bale is typically sold as *two-string* or *three-string*. Two-string bales weigh 50 to 60 pounds (23 to 27 kilograms) and measure about 36 inches long x 18 inches wide x 14 inches high (91 x 45 x 36 centimeters). Three-string bales weigh 75 to 80 pounds (34 to 36 kilograms) and measure about 42 x 23 x 16 inches (107 x 60 x 40 centimeters). I recommend that you use two-string bales for this project because they're lighter in weight and therefore easier to maneuver than three-string bales.

Instructions

This simple structure uses five two-string bales to form three sides of a single-layer, open-sided bin. Its rectangular interior composting area is about 3 feet wide x 4½ feet long x 14 inches high (1 meter x 1.3 meters x 36 centimeters).

1. **Place two bales end to end to form one side wall that measures 6 feet (1.8 meters) long.**

2. **Place one bale perpendicular to the first wall as the back wall.**

3. **Place the remaining two bales end to end to form the third wall.**

One more bale completes the rectangle if you prefer to keep your compost contained in an enclosed bin. Set it against the outer edges of the side walls, making it easier to swing outward if you want to open the enclosure.

Another option for this bin is to stack another five bales for a second layer, increasing the height to 28 inches (71 centimeters) and providing you with more composting space. This design helps your heap self-insulate and retain more heat and moisture.

If you're building your bin higher than two layers, offset bales with the layer below when stacking to create greater stability.

Use straw bales to create temporary composting sites. Surround the area where you want to add a garden in a year or two with straw bales and compost within them to improve the soil beneath. As the straw decomposes, work it into your compost, and as the compost decomposes, work it into the soil. By the time you're ready to plant, you'll be plunging your shovel into rich, dark soil and your "bin" will have disappeared, leaving you with nothing to move or store.

Stacking up concrete blocks for bins

Concrete blocks are easy to work with if you want to build a single bin and add more sections as your composting needs increase or more blocks become available. Fewer blocks are needed to build the second (or third) bin because they share a common wall.

If you enjoy practicing the 3 Rs (Reduce, Reuse, Recycle), you may be able to find free concrete blocks here and there until you accumulate enough to build your bin. Ask friends, neighbors, or contractors with renovation projects if they have leftovers. Does your town periodically offer free trash collection days when they accept any and all refuse, no matter how cumbersome? I'm always astounded at the piles of perfectly serviceable construction materials that I see dumped curbside in my city on those days. Put an advertisement in your local paper or on Web sites such as www.craigslist.org or www.freecycle.org. Many people donate items to anyone who will haul them away.

Level the ground where you plan to stack your concrete blocks, lay them out in your desired arrangement and to meet your desired bin height, and then use a hammer or mallet to drive metal posts through the holes in the blocks into the ground to provide stability. The following figure gives you an idea of how your bin may look. You can also easily add a second or third adjacent bin.

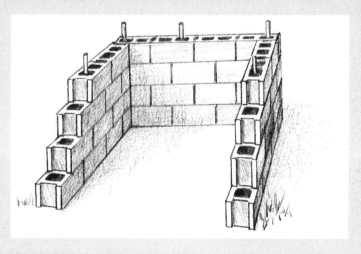

Wood and wire three-bin composter

A stationary wood and wire three-bin system (see Figure 6-3) is a style that offers a variety of advantages, including that you can compost large amounts of yard materials in relatively little time. Wire mesh sides and/or bottoms keep pests out of the bin while allowing the aeration needed for decomposition, and the wood construction blends unobtrusively for a natural appearance in your landscape. You can also fabricate pest-proof hinged lids from wood and wire or fiberglass. (A fiberglass lid maintains moisture within the pile or keeps out excessive rain or snow, depending on your conditions.)

Building this bin style yourself requires more carpentry skills and tools than other projects in this chapter, and the materials are more expensive than other home-built styles. You can build this unit for approximately $300 to $375.

This bin design and construction project is courtesy of Seattle Public Utilities. The overall outside dimension of the finished project is 9 feet wide x 3 feet deep x 32 inches high (approximately 2.7 meters x 1 meter x 0.8 meters); each bin section measures 35½ inches wide x 3 feet deep x 32 inches high (approximately 1 meter x 1 meter x 0.8 meters). You can downsize the design to a one- or two-bin system if that's all the space you require. (Flip back to Chapter 5 for an overview of how adjacent bins help your composting efforts.) For instructions for building other types of composting bins, visit www.seattletilth.org, or use your favorite Internet search engine to find instructions for other designs.

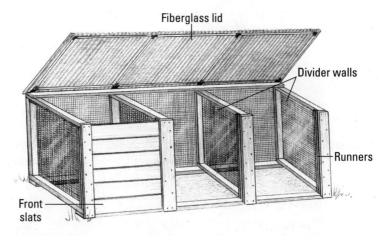

Figure 6-3: A wood and wire three-bin system with a fiberglass lid.

Materials and tools

The list of materials and tools needed to construct the three-bin composter is lengthy, but you should be able to find everything you need at a home improvement store.

- Two 18-foot cedar 2 x 4s
- Four 12-foot (or eight 6-foot) cedar 2 x 4s
- One 9-foot 2 x 2
- Two 6-foot 2 x 2s
- One 16-foot cedar 2 x 6
- Nine 6-foot cedar 1 x 6s
- 22 feet of 36-inch-wide ½-inch hardware cloth
- 12 ½-inch carriage bolts, 4 inches long
- 12 washers and 12 nuts for bolts
- 3 pounds of 16d galvanized nails
- ½ pound of 8d galvanized casement nails
- 250 poultry wire staples or power stapler
- 12-foot sheet of 4-ounce clear corrugated fiberglass
- 8-foot sheet of 4-ounce clear corrugated fiberglass
- Three 8-foot lengths of wiggle molding
- 40 gasketed aluminum nails
- Two 3-inch zinc-plated hinges
- 8 flat 4-corner braces with screws
- 4 flat 3-inch T-braces with screws

This project requires the following tools:

- Hand saw or circular power saw
- Drill with ½-inch and ⅛-inch bits
- Screwdriver
- Hammer or power stapler with 1-inch-long galvanized staples
- Tin snips
- Tape measure
- Pencil
- ¾ socket or open-ended wrench

✔ Carpenter's square

✔ Safety glasses

✔ Ear protection

Instructions

The following steps walk you through building the three-bin composter, starting with the dividers and finishing with the fiberglass lid.

1. **Cut two 31½-inch and two 36-inch pieces from each 12-foot 2 x 4.**

2. **Butt end nail the four pieces into a 35-x-36-inch divider section (see Figure 6-4). Check to make sure each divider section is square.**

3. **Repeat Step 2 for the other three divider sections.**

4. **Cut four 37-inch-long sections of hardware cloth and bend back the edges 1 inch. Stretch across each divider frame, check for squareness of the frame, and staple the screen tightly into place every 4 inches around the edge.**

5. **Set the dividers up parallel to one another 3 feet apart.**

6. **Measure and mark the centers of the two inside dividers.**

7. **Cut four 9-foot pieces out of the two 18-foot 2 x 4 boards.**

8. **Place two 9-foot base boards on top of the dividers and measure the positions for the two inside dividers.**

9. **Mark a centerline for each divider on the 9-foot 2 x 4. With each divider, line up the centerlines and make the baseboard flush against the outer edge of the divider.**

Figure 6-4: Align corners to butt end nail them together.

10. Drill a ½-inch hole through each junction centered 1-inch in from the inside edge. Secure baseboards with carriage bolts, but don't tighten them yet.

11. Turn the unit right side up and repeat Steps 9 and 10 for the top 9-foot board.

12. Using the carpenter's square or measuring between opposing corners, make sure the bin is square, and tighten all bolts securely.

13. Fasten a 9-foot-long piece of hardware cloth securely to the backside of the bin with staples every 4 inches around the frame.

14. Cut four 36-inch long 2 x 6s for front slat runners.

15. Cut two of the boards from Step 14 lengthwise to 4¾-inches wide and nail them securely to the front of the two outside dividers and baseboard, making them flush on the top and outside edges.

    Save the remainder of the rip cut boards from this step for use as back runners.

16. Center the remaining 36-inch, full-width 2 x 6 boards on the front of the inside dividers flush with the top edge, and nail securely.

17. To create back runners, cut the remaining 2 x 6 into a 34-inch long piece and then rip cut it into four equal pieces, 1¼ x 2 inches. Nail the back runner parallel to the front runners on the side of each divider, leaving a 1-inch gap for slats.

18. Cut all the 1 x 6-inch cedar boards into slats 31¼-inches long.

19. Use the last 9-foot 2 x 4 for the back of the lid. Cut four 32½-inch 2 x 2s and one 9-foot 2 x 2 from it.

20. Lay the pieces from Step 19 on the ground in a rectangle and make sure they're square. Screw in corner braces and T-braces on the bottom side of the frame.

21. Center the lid frame from Step 20 on the bin structure, brace side down, and attach it to the bin with the hinges.

22. Cut wiggle board to fit the front and back 9-foot sections of the lid frame.

23. Pre-drill the wiggle board with a ⅛-inch drill bit, and nail it to the frame with 8d casement nails.

24. Cut the fiberglass to fit flush with the front and back edges of the frame.

25. Overlay the fiberglass pieces at least one channel wide. Pre-drill the fiberglass and wiggle board for each nail hole.

26. Nail the fiberglass and wiggle board to the lid frame, nailing on top of every third corrugated hump with gasketed nails.

Dressing up your concrete block bins

The concrete block composting bins covered in the sidebar "Stacking up concrete blocks for bins" are pretty bare-bones and not much to look at. But you can take your concrete block unit a few steps further and make it functional *and* fashionable! Here are some ideas for making your concrete construction piece more pleasing to the eye:

✔ Purchase slightly more expensive blocks with integrated designs or terra-cotta colors meant to blend in with landscaping projects.

✔ Fill a few of the top layer of block holes with soil, toss in a few seeds, and see what happens. (Of course, you'll have to monitor the plants' water and nutrient needs.)

✔ Plant a vine at the outside base of the bin. Use a clinging vine with tendrils that grip the block surface on their upward climb, or attach poultry wire or a trellis to support growth. Be forewarned: Vines can grow like crazy and romp across the entire bin if you don't keep them in check!

✔ Paint or stucco (or render, for my readers in the United Kingdom) the blocks to blend in with your home's other architectural features.

✔ Tile the outside with a mosaic design or unleash your kids or grandkids to paint a mural on the sides. For tiny tikes, paint a giant ruler on the wall to track their growth.

✔ Hide the bin with a portable lattice screen. Lattice panels come in wood or plastic composite. Plastic tends to hold up better with less maintenance than wood in outdoor conditions.

✔ Attach natural reed or bamboo screening to the exterior. Screening is available in rolls of various lengths and widths.

Part III
Compost Happens

The 5th Wave   By Rich Tennant

In this part . . .

Dig into this part to unearth the nitty-gritty of concocting compost. If you read only this part of the book, you'll know everything necessary to make and use rich, organic compost.

You can't make compost without the right ingredients, so I describe the different organic materials to put in your compost as well as what to keep out of it. You come to understand the factors that go into constructing an efficient compost pile, such as moisture content and aeration. Sets of step-by-step composting instructions are geared to how much time and effort you want to expend. And finally, you discover uses for your lovely finished compost in myriad gardening and landscaping activities.

Chapter 7

Selecting Your Ingredients

*A*ll once-living things decompose eventually, so you may wonder whether it really matters what goes into your compost heap or how much material you use. If you're in no hurry to obtain useable compost, you don't have to be too concerned about those issues — compost happens. But if you're a gardener who wants lots of crumbly compost sooner rather than later, understanding the basic hows and whys of selecting carbon-rich and nitrogen-rich organic matter and mixing them in the right proportion is invaluable.

This chapter defines the different organic materials available to put in your compost pile and helps you figure out the best proportions of each. It also covers all the stuff that should definitely stay out of your pile! Finally, lots of ideas on finding free ingredients (and storing them) leave you no excuses for running out of organic matter!

Getting Down with Browns: Carbon-Rich Ingredients

Gardeners who compost often refer to carbon-rich materials as *browns* because most of them are various shades of brown. Sugar-rich carbon materials provide energy for microorganisms while they busily break down your organic matter. Carbons for the compost pile (in order of general availability for most folks) include dry leaves, woody plant trimmings, all sorts of paper products, straw, pine needles, and sawdust.

Dry leaves

Dry leaves are probably the easiest brown ingredient to work with for a beginning composter because they're already smallish pieces of organic matter that are easy to shred into even tinier pieces if you choose. They're also in abundant supply in most regions and turn into fairly decent finished compost (called *leaf mold*) all by themselves, without the addition of other materials. Just take a look at any woodland floor to see how it happens. The nearby side-bar "When life gives you leaves, make leaf mold" tells you how to work with lots of leaves to create moisture-enhancing compost.

Shredding leaves reduces their volume, making it easier to stock-pile large quantities to add to your compost as needed. Shred leaves by spreading them across the grass and running over them with a lawn mower. No lawn and mower? Fill a plastic garbage can half full of leaves and rattle a weed eater in it as a leaf shredder. (Be sure to wear protective eye gear.)

When life gives you leaves, make leaf mold

If you have lots of leaves but are low on other organic matter to mix with them, create *leaf mold.* Like compost, finished leaf mold is dark and crumbly with a pleasing earthy aroma. Although leaf mold doesn't contain as much nutritional value as compost for improving soil fertility, it does a good job of enhancing soil's ability to retain moisture.

The process is the same as building a compost heap, minus the variety in ingredients. You decide how much labor to put in, and as with any composting effort, the smaller the original pieces and the more you turn and add water as needed, the faster the decomposition rate. It takes about 6 to 24 months to obtain leaf mold with either of these methods:

✔ Pile leaves (shredded or whole) in a heap or in a bin at least 3 cubic feet (1 cubic meter) in size. Moisten the leaves as you work, dampening everything until it's like a wrung-out sponge. Turn and remoisten (or not) periodically just as you would a compost heap.

✔ Fill a heavy-duty plastic garbage bag with shredded, moistened leaves, and tie the bag tightly. Make a few slits in the bag to allow airflow or it will become a stinky, anaerobic system. Flop the bag around frequently (or not) to mix and introduce air. Untie and add water as needed.

The truth about toxic leaves

No matter where you garden, there seems to be at least one plant whose leaves are rumored to have toxic potential in the compost pile. Here's the lowdown on several common concerns that pop up again and again:

✔ **Black walnut:** Black walnut trees *(Juglanas nigra)* produce a chemical called juglone that inhibits growth of some plant species in the surrounding area, although other plant species are tolerant of juglone. (Detailed lists of juglone-tolerant and -intolerant plant species are available online and in many plant-related gardening books.) Composting black walnut leaves in an actively managed compost pile is safe because the juglone breaks down and loses toxicity within 2 to 4 weeks. If you're unconvinced, test your compost by planting a few tomato seedlings in it. Tomatoes are highly susceptible to juglone, so if they survive, your compost is fine! Just don't use uncomposted black walnut leaves or other litter from the tree as mulch.

✔ **Eucalyptus:** Although information has been passed around for years stating that eucalyptus leaves are bad for compost, researchers have determined that there's no evidence that plant growth is inhibited by "yuke" leaves in the compost. This rumor may have started because some eucalyptus species have aggressive roots and drop tremendous amounts of litter that make competition difficult for other plants.

✔ **Oleander:** All parts of this evergreen shrub *(Oleander nerium)* are poisonous and may be fatal if ingested, but there's no proof that its toxicity hinders a final compost product. Researchers found that the toxin *oleandrin* broke down rapidly in the first 50 days in a compost pile and after 300 days, it was undetectable. Other plant roots don't absorb the toxin either. However, use caution when working with oleander material because it exudes sap that may cause skin and eye inflammations and allergic reactions in some people. I witnessed this at a composting demonstration when a young woman's bare arms and legs erupted into painful red welts within minutes after she moved a pile of grass clippings that contained bits of oleander trimmings. Wear gloves, a dust mask, safety glasses, and long sleeves and pants if working with oleander. Never run oleander through a shredder because you could inhale microscopic bits of plant dust.

Woody plant trimmings

Shrubs, trees, palm fronds, dead perennial stems, Brussels sprout stalks, and dried cornstalks all fit into this category. Break, chop, and shred this material as much as possible to speed decomposition. (Chapter 2 describes tools that help with this.) However, if you can't chop it really small, don't worry; there's nothing wrong with pulling partially decomposed twigs and branches from a finished compost pile to add to a new pile (perhaps multiple times) until they're completely "gone." Another use for woody materials: Spread them at the bottom of a pile before construction to promote aeration.

 Get a few of your neighbors together and arrange to tackle your pruning chores at the same time. Pile up all your woody trimmings, and then convene for a shredding party. Rent a chipper/shredder from a tool rental store, and share the cost, labor, and results.

Paper products

Although I try to recycle as much of my paper as possible, plenty is still left for composting. I particularly like to use shredded paper for worm bin bedding, which you can find out more about in Chapter 10. Other paper products that are easy to shred or tear include used paper towels, envelopes, paperboard (unwaxed cereal and food boxes), paper towel and toilet tissue rolls, and newspaper.

Cardboard is slow to compost, and the thicker corrugated stuff is hard to tear, although it works well for soaking up excess moisture in wet ingredients. Tear it and mix it with fresh manure or grass clippings, or lay it on the bottom of a pile if you're composting in a damp region. Check out Chapter 12 for another easy way to recycle cardboard's organic content by creating rich garden soil with layers of cardboard and other organic materials.

 Cardboard is easier to deal with if you leave it lying around for a few days when the weather is damp; then it tears easily, and the dampness also allows you to easily remove any packing tape rather than pulling all those annoying bits out of your finished compost later.

Straw

Made from the remaining dried stalks of cereal grains (wheat, oats, rye, barley) after the grain has been threshed and removed, straw is used primarily for livestock bedding. It's used less frequently than hay as livestock feed because straw's nutritional value and digestibility are low. (See the section "Hay" later in this chapter to compare the two.) You can use straw in the garden as mulch; it's safer to use than hay because it contains few weed seeds.

Pine needles

The resinous coating on needles can take a while to break down, so use them in limited quantity. If you have a lot of pine needles, you can easily stockpile them and gradually mix them in with other organic materials. (Pine needles also make attractive and effective mulch spread around garden beds.) Don't worry about pine needles' acidity unless you have a lot of them: Small amounts have minimal effect in your compost pile or soil.

Sawdust

Because sawdust has an extremely high carbon to nitrogen (or C:N) ratio (more about that later in the chapter), use it sparingly in the compost pile. Sandwich an ultra-thin layer (no more than an inch) between moist grass clippings, or mix handfuls thoroughly with lots of other ingredients.

Thick layers of sawdust compress into impenetrable mats, reducing the ability of oxygen and water to circulate through the pile. Also, decomposers start to work on sawdust as they do every other ingredient, but because of the high carbon load, they require copious amounts of nitrogen-rich material over time to process all that carbon. Sprinkling small amounts of sawdust you generate in your woodshop won't hurt the process; dumping huge amounts from the local sawmill will shut it down.

Try these alternative uses if you have access to lots of sawdust:

- ✔ Spread it as mulch on pathways.

- ✔ Layer it as mulch to kill weeds.

- ✔ Stockpile it by itself in a holding area to decompose for a year or more. Adding it to compost piles as a carbon source then is safer.

Greening It Up: Nitrogen-Rich Ingredients

Nitrogen-rich materials are called *greens* because most of them are greenish in color. Of course, there are usually exceptions to any rule just to keep you on your toes. Manure and coffee grounds are nitrogen materials that happen to be brown. Greens provide body-building proteins for the microorganisms crunching through your organic matter. Good green sources include kitchen scraps, grass clippings, leafy plant trimmings, and manure. Feathers, fur, and hair are other nitrogen sources to use.

Kitchen scraps

Other than items listed in the section "Knowing which Materials to Avoid" later in this chapter, leftovers from the kitchen are excellent additions to the compost pile. You do the environment a big favor too, because kitchen waste not only fills up scarce landfill sites, but it also produces methane, a greenhouse gas, as it decomposes. In the bargain, you also save resources needed to transport and process that waste by adding the following scraps to your compost:

✔ Coffee grounds and used filters

✔ Condiments and sauces

✔ Corncobs

✔ Cut flowers

✔ Eggshells

✔ Fruit pits

✔ Fruit rinds and cores

✔ Nut shells

✔ Shells from shellfish

✔ Stale or moldy bread and grain products

✔ Tea and tea bags

✔ Vegetables (raw or cooked)

Fruit pits, eggshells, nut shells, and shellfish shells are slow to decompose. Crush or grind them before adding them to your compost pile, in order to speed the process.

Some local municipalities may have restrictions on adding food waste to open compost bins, although covered or enclosed bins are usually okay. Check for restrictions in your area.

Grass clippings

If I had to pick a favorite composting ingredient, it would likely be grass clippings. Pre-chopped into tiny pieces by the mower and loaded with moisture and nitrogen, what's not to like? Oh, I almost forgot: Grass clippings turn slimy and smelly if left in big piles or layered too thickly, so mix them up with brown materials as soon as possible or spread them out to dry for a few hours before mixing them into your heap.

If organic gardening principles are important to you, and the clippings you use originate from neighbors or other sources, verify that the lawns weren't treated with chemical fertilizers or herbicides.

If you don't need your grass clippings for composting, *grasscycling* is an easy recycling alternative. All you have to do is let the clippings lie on the lawn after mowing! Clippings decompose quickly and return up to 25 percent of the total nutrients your lawn requires, meaning you can apply 25 percent less fertilizer to your lawn. A mower with a mulching feature will reduce the size of grass clippings, speeding decomposition.

Leafy plant trimmings, spent flowers, herbs, and vegetables

When your garden plants have finished producing for the season, pull them out, chop or tear them into smaller pieces, and toss them into the compost pile to recycle their nitrogen content. The same goes for leafy trimmings from landscape shrubs and trees. If plants exhibit pest or disease problems, it's better to leave them out of the compost mix (see "Knowing which Materials to Avoid" later in this chapter).

If bracken ferns have spread invasively in your garden or landscape, the greenery makes an excellent addition to the compost heap when you cut it early in the growing season. Don't add the roots, though, as this tough plant can be a problem in gardens. However, aim to finish harvesting bracken ferns for your pile by early summer, as by mid to late summer the leaves have produced spores that can be harmful when inhaled.

Weeds — foliage only!

A healthy crop of weeds, although annoying, is a fine source of nitrogen. Return those nutrients to your garden where they belong by composting your weeds. Be sure you don't include seed heads or perennial roots that may sprout.

Livestock manure

Chicken, cow, duck, geese, goat, horse, llama, rabbit, sheep, and turkey manures are safe to add to compost. Manure contains very small amounts of macronutrients (nitrogen, phosphorus, and potassium) that all plants require, as well as essential micronutrients (trace elements), such as boron, iron, and zinc. Although manure adds only marginally to the overall nutrient level of your compost, it does provide significant organic matter and loads of microbial activity.

Depending on the animals' diet, some manures may contain a lot of weed seeds, so if you're obtaining a load of manure straight from the source (so to speak), inquire about the animal's feeding habits. (See the later section, "Hay.") Horse manure, in particular, can be loaded with seeds that pass through the animal's digestive system. Unless you compost with a *hot pile* that reaches temperatures above 131 degrees Fahrenheit (55 degrees Celsius) for 72 hours (see Chapter 8), seeds may survive composting and sprout, becoming a nuisance in the garden.

If you're using manure directly on your garden, it must be at least six months old to be safe. Fresh manure, in addition to being smelly, contains concentrated nitrogen that may "burn" plant roots and tender seedlings or prevent seed germination. (Yellow dog spots on your lawn are a visual example of the potency of nitrogen-rich waste.) You can add fresh manure straight onto your compost heap because it's nitrogen-rich, hot, and moisture-laden. However, it can throw off the workings of a compost pile if added in abundant quantities. If you happen to obtain super-fresh wet manure, use it in the following ways:

- ✔ Let it dry out a little before adding it to your compost, and then blend it sparingly with a wide variety of other ingredients.
- ✔ Compost it in a pile by itself.
- ✔ Spread fresh manure across garden beds in fall, allowing it to rot during the winter months.
- ✔ Spread it across beds that *lie fallow* (that is, that aren't used for growing anything) six months to one year before planting.

Digging manure into the top layer of soil promotes speedier decomposition. Never spread fresh manure on a garden that is already planted, because its "heat" can kill plants. Nor do you want it to splash onto edible foliage. How long to wait before planting depends on the freshness of the manure and how quickly it decomposes in your climate.

Always wear protective gear (gloves and shoes, as well as a dust mask if the manure is dry and dusty) when collecting or spreading manure. And no matter how protected you are, good hygiene is still absolutely essential: Be sure to wash your hands thoroughly and scrub under your nails after handling manure.

Manure obtained in bulk from farms, stables, and animal owners (as opposed to the kind you get in a plastic bag from the garden center) may contain more than just nitrogen-rich material. Mixed in may be carbon-rich bedding materials, such as straw or sawdust. That's absolutely fine — it's a compost pile in process even before you return home with the goods!

Pet bedding

Small pets such as hamsters, rabbits, guinea pigs, and gerbils are bedded down with newspaper, hay, and/or shavings, and this used bedding is a very useful addition to the compost heap.

Feathers

When I was a little kid playing softball, a teammate's dad spread a layer of chicken feathers (his family raised eggs for sale) over our infield in late fall. Chicken feathers fluttered around in a surreal snowfall until real snow packed them down for the winter. I can't prove that it helped my team win any games, but the following spring, we played on the lushest, greenest, most enviable grass of any team in the region.

 If you don't live near or have access to a poultry farm, you can empty any unwanted feather pillows, down comforters, or feather-filled cushions in your home and mix in the feathers as you fill your compost bin.

Hair and fur

Clean your hairbrush (and Fido's and Fluffy's) over the compost bin. If you're desperate for nitrogen, ask your friendly barber, stylist, or pet groomer to save you a stash when they sweep up. Hair and fur can take a while to disintegrate if piles aren't maintained to actively decompose.

Hay

Bales of hay are comprised of legumes and grasses, such as alfalfa, red clover, or timothy, that are grown as feed for livestock. Foliage is cut when still green and left to dry in the field until machines compress it into rectangular bales. To maintain its nutritional value for animals and to prevent spoilage, hay must dry uniformly and quickly, with limited exposure to sun and rain. Nitrogen content varies depending upon the plants grown (legumes like alfalfa and clover contain more nitrogen than grasses) and the drying process. A concern to consider before adding hay to your compost pile is its weed content.

Depending on where and how hay is grown and processed, it may contain a bumper crop of weed seeds that survive the compost pile to sprout in your garden. If you don't know the source and the hay isn't certified as weed-free, seek alternative forms of nitrogen for your compost.

Using the Right Ratio of Carbon to Nitrogen Ingredients

You may hear the C:N ratio bandied about in discussions among avid composters. As Chapter 3 describes in detail, decomposers that actively break down organic matter prefer a diet containing about 30 times the amount of carbon-rich material as nitrogen-rich material, or a C:N ratio of 30:1. The closer you can come to mixing up 3 parts carbon materials to one part nitrogen materials when you build your pile, the faster the decomposers will consume it and reward you with finished compost.

Actual carbon and nitrogen content in material varies, but typical ranges are included in Table 7-1. Use them as a guide to figure proportions of browns and greens when you're mixing up a batch of compost, but don't stress over precision measurements. Blending carbon and nitrogen ingredients in the "low to middle ranges" of the C:N ratio (such as dry leaves and grass clippings) is a good starting point. Use high-carbon materials (such as cardboard and sawdust) sparingly. After you construct a few piles, you'll get the hang of mixing up your available greens and browns in appropriate amounts.

Combine one part nitrogen materials with three parts carbon materials to achieve the 30:1 carbon to nitrogen ratio.

Juicing up the process

A somewhat bewildering array of products with names like accelerators, activators, and inoculators are available for sale. Their purpose is to speed up the decomposition process and/or enhance the finished product. Most research studies show that they're unnecessary because the ingredients that are essential to achieve a good-quality finished product — nitrogen, carbon, water, and air — already exist in a well-constructed compost pile. Monikers of these products are often used interchangeably, but if you're interested in experimenting, here are the products' basic characteristics:

✔ **Accelerators:** They jumpstart the decomposition process by adding nitrogen in some form, and they may also contain bacteria, enzymes, or other ingredients.

Mix a shovel or two of either local soil or finished compost from your last pile into your new pile for an accelerator that's as effective as any you can buy. Natural materials that make excellent compost accelerators include nettles (the tops, not the roots) and comfrey.

✔ **Activators:** These contain nitrogen and are usually added to "activate" a pile that is slow to decompose. Activators that you buy are of two types: those derived from chemical sources, such as ammonium nitrate fertilizer, and those from natural sources, such as protein meals (alfalfa, blood, corn, cottonseed, or soybean), seaweed, or pelleted chicken manure. I don't recommend chemical nitrogen fertilizers as activators. They don't last long in the pile, may harm beneficial microorganisms and earthworms, and provide no protein, which microorganisms require to work and reproduce. Also, chemical fertilizers may become a source of water pollution if they leach out of the pile.

If your pile decomposition rate slows because of a lack of nitrogen, the best solution is to turn it and incorporate more green materials. If you don't have access to sufficient greens, go ahead and try the natural activators listed in the preceding paragraph. Understand, however, that this is usually a temporary fix, because the pile heats up quickly and then decomposition slows right back down if you can't incorporate more bulky green matter to keep it running.

High-nitrogen plant meals are less costly if purchased in pellet form in big bags from farm and feed supply stores rather than as powdered meal in small containers at the garden center. In a pinch, a bag of dried dog food (loaded with corn) works as an activator.

✔ **Inoculators:** Typically comprised of specific dormant bacteria, fungi, or other microorganisms, inoculators are supposed to speed decomposition or produce better-quality compost. It's unlikely that you'll ever need to add more critters, because the organic matter in your pile and the soil beneath it are already teeming with indigenous life forms eager to do the job.

Table 7-1	Carbon to Nitrogen Ratios		
Carbon-Rich Ingredients	**Carbon to Nitrogen Ratio***	**Nitrogen-Rich Ingredients**	**Carbon to Nitrogen Ratio***
Corn stalks	60:1	Chicken manure	10:1
Corrugated cardboard	600:1	Coffee grounds	20:1
Dry leaves	40–80:1	Garden plants and weeds	20–35:1
Mixed paper products	200–800:1	Grass clippings	10–25:1
Newspaper	150–200:1	Hay	10–25:1
Pine needles	60–110:1	Kitchen scraps	10–50:1
Sawdust, weathered 3 years	142:1	Rotted manure	20–50:1
Sawdust, weathered 2 months	625:1		
Straw	50–150:1		
Woody plant trimmings	200–1,300:1		

* Representative ranges only. Actual carbon to nitrogen ratio varies depending on such factors as plant species and material composition.

Knowing which Materials to Avoid

Composting isn't a free-for-all. You can't toss in anything and everything you come across waste-wise and expect it to produce usable, healthy compost. Some materials definitely don't qualify as compost ingredients because they contain pathogens, attract pests, or cause other problems. Save yourself hassles and headaches by keeping the following items out of your composting operation:

 ✔ **Meat, bones, grease, fats, oils, or dairy products:** They turn rancid and smelly, and attract dogs, cats, raccoons, foxes, and rodents.

✔ **Feces:** Waste from dogs, cats (including soiled cat litter), pet birds, pigs, and humans may contain parasites that are transferable to and infectious for humans.

✔ **Charcoal barbecue or coal ashes:** All gardeners should leave these alone because they contain sulfur oxides and other chemicals you don't want to transfer to your garden.

✔ **Wood ashes:** Wood ashes are alkaline. If you garden where soils are alkaline (like much of the western and southwestern United States) you don't want to increase alkalinity by adding ashes to your compost mix. However, if you garden where soils are acidic, wood ashes can be added in small amounts. Sprinkle handfuls throughout as you mix a pile.

✔ **Treated wood products:** Don't add wood chips or sawdust from chemically treated or pressure-treated wood.

If you become a serious composting enthusiast who likes to monitor and maintain hot piles, the following three items can be composted. Monitoring your pile's temperature and turning it frequently are essential. (See Chapter 8 for details.) If you describe yourself as a laid-back, "compost happens" gardening guy or gal, you're better off safe than sorry. Dispose of these problem-prone plant materials in the trash:

✔ Weeds with seed heads. You can pull weeds before they go to seed and toss them in your compost pile as a good source of nitrogen. But if seeds have set, toss the entire plant in the trash.

✔ Disease- or insect-infested plant material.

✔ Plants that spread with invasive root systems, such as African couch grass, Bermuda grass, bindweed, Canada thistle and other thistles, dock weed, morning glory, and nettle. Just a smidgen of this root material can survive to sprout another day and spread havoc throughout your garden.

If throwing away organic matter, no matter how weedy and disease-ridden, sends minor guilt pangs up and down your spine but you don't have time to regularly maintain a hot pile, stockpile all the bad stuff in a separate bin where it can't inadvertently be mixed in with the good stuff. Or place all the bad stuff in a large (30- to 40-gallon), black, thick plastic garbage bag and seal it. When the quantity is sufficient and you have plenty of green, nitrogen-rich materials (such as grass clippings or manure) to add to it, build one pile to neutralize the problems. Laboring over just one hot heap per garden season isn't as time-consuming as ensuring that every pile heats up to the red zone.

Another option is to take diseased or invasive plant material to your local recycling center that collects green waste. Ask if they compost at sufficiently high temperatures to destroy your problem plants. If they do, make your contribution; if they don't, it's back to Plan A.

Getting Your Hands on Compostable Materials

If you have insufficient carbon or nitrogen to whip up a good mix of materials, you can wait to build a compost pile until your landscape generates what you need, stockpiling what you do have in the meantime. Or, you can take charge and go on a hunt for what you want. You may be pleasantly surprised at the wide availability of materials just waiting for someone to claim them. This section offers tips on both stockpiling what you have and tracking down more, so that, in the end, you have the best compost on the block.

Stockpiling your own organic matter

Your landscape may generate significant amounts of materials at different times of the year. Rather than bemoaning all those fallen leaves that must be raked in autumn, consider them a wonderful abundance of carbon-rich material that you can stockpile for a year's worth of composting experiments. Because dry carbon materials seldom, if ever, generate bad odors, they're easy to store. You may want to have a separate holding unit for carbon materials, including leaves, straw, sawdust, and chipped plant material. Pick up curbside plastic bags full of leaves in your neighborhood, and pile them in an out-of-sight corner of the yard.

Too much of a good thing

Large quantities of high-carbon materials, such as sawdust, straw, or shredded newspaper, invite soil microorganisms to dive into the buffet, and the wealth of food allows them to reproduce in great quantities. However, their burgeoning population also requires nitrogen for bodybuilding, so they tie up existing nitrogen in the soil, which is called *nitrogen immobilization*. After the critters perform their role, nitrogen will be released again as they die off.

Unfortunately, this process may negatively impact your garden in the short term because nitrogen is one of three essential nutrients (along with phosphorus and potassium) for healthy plant development. Without nitrogen, your plants may look stunted or yellow. If you have a load of high-carbon organic matter, stockpile it for gradual use, mixing small quantities into the compost pile.

Green, nitrogen-rich material is more problematic to stockpile because it usually has a high moisture content and can become stinky and matted or attract flies. Spread grass clippings out thinly to dry a bit rather than leaving them in a big pile, but try to use them quickly because their moisture is an advantage in the compost pile. A pile of fresh manure loses its odor within a couple weeks. Stockpile it in an out-of-the-way locale where you can plunder it as needed. Finally, if you find yourself with a load of green garden waste at the end of the season, chopping it up into compostable pieces when it's fresh is easier than waiting until it dries out and becomes stringy and/or woody.

Rounding up free organic matter

Suppose your composting mania kicks into high gear, but your landscape and household can't generate as much organic matter as you need. Plenty of free organic matter is in need of a good home! Various materials and sources include

- ✔ **Free leaves:** Walk around your neighborhood and see who puts out bags of lawn clippings or dried leaves for trash pickup or green waste collection. In autumn, look out for work crews clearing leaves from the street and collect some for yourself. If local pickup fees are based on volume, neighbors may be so delighted by your interest in composting that they'll haul their bags of leaves to your house! I know an avid young composting family whose neighbors drop off bags of trimmings in their driveway on the way to work, giving a friendlier meaning to the term "drive-by dumping."

Express your appreciation for the free organic matter by dropping off a basket of juicy tomatoes or a bouquet of fresh-cut flowers from your garden. Not only is it a neighborly gesture, but it also shows tangible results of what happened to all that "useless" rotting organic matter. Your contact may become a composting convert.

- ✔ **Coffee grounds:** Not only does java provide nitrogen, but used grounds are already tiny and moisture-laden to promote speedy decomposition. Check with your neighborhood cafe or 24-hour restaurants near freeway exits. They brew umpteen pots of coffee to keep all those drivers awake!

- ✔ **Manure:** Ask local farmers, stables, and dairies. Large operations typically have waste management systems in place to deal with all that bulk, so you may be luckier with small operations or family farms. In urban areas, check neighborhoods known as *horse properties,* where residents have space for a few horses, goats, or chickens.

✔ **Regional by-products:** What food or fiber products are grown and processed in your area? Think apple mash at cider factories, hops from microbreweries, grape skins from wineries, and cottonseed hulls from cotton gins.

✔ **Grocery stores and markets:** Produce departments trim and cull fruits and vegetables daily. Their in-store delis may be a source of coffee grounds.

✔ **Landscape maintenance companies:** Check the Yellow Pages or watch your neighborhood for local companies that regularly handle mowing and trimming projects. They pay fees to dump clippings and trimmings at the landfill. Because they also factor in the expense of gas, wear and tear on trucks, and employee time spent driving to landfills, most are delighted to deposit a load of organic matter in your driveway. Discuss the contents with them in advance if you need green grass clippings or brown dried leaves. Be sure you don't get a load of diseased plants, poisonous oleander leaves, or thorny rose bush trimmings! Also, discuss the pesticide and chemical fertilizers used with the landscape supervisor. She may be able to steer the "truly organic" matter to you.

✔ **Utilities:** Electric companies trim trees beneath utility wires. They typically work with a heavy-duty chipper/shredder, so they're an excellent source for bark chips. The downside is that there's often a waiting list, and they may not schedule a drop far in advance.

✔ **Local municipalities:** You may be lucky to live in a community that runs a waste-reduction project that includes drop-off/pick-up points for organic matter. Drop off your dried leaves in fall and pick up a batch of compost. Such a deal! Check with local waste management departments, parks and recreation services, garden clubs, or cooperative extension offices to find programs in your area.

 Place a request for organic matter on the Internet through your local Craigslist (www.craigslist.org) or Freecycle (www.freecycle.org) listings. Also post fliers with your requests at local shops, your library, and other similar spots in your area.

Chapter 8

Mixing Up a Batch: A Step-by-Step Guide

In This Chapter

▶ Deciding where to locate your compost area

▶ Mixing and maintaining a pile

▶ Figuring out when it's done

▶ Refining your composting style

I'm willing to bet there are as many composting techniques as there are gardeners, but following a few basic guidelines makes the process easy for beginners. (And if you prove that composting can be easy, you have a better chance of getting family and friends to join in!) This chapter ushers you through the nuts and bolts of placing, creating, and maintaining a compost pile. I also offer pointers to help you fine-tune your composting style after you have the basics covered.

Deciding on Location

You've decided to get into the composting game. Way to go! First you need to figure out a good location in your landscape to situate your composting efforts. I offer some practical considerations in this section, but only you can decide those all-important "aesthetic issues" if, for example, you're dealing with folks who aren't enthusiastic about rotting organic matter in their line of sight. You may take pride in pointing out your elegantly designed, three-bin composting operation to guests from the living room window, but if your housemate is mortified, that's probably not a good location. (It could also be a sign that you're not living with a compatible housemate, but that's another book entirely!)

To be a good neighbor, take into account your neighbors' views or potential concerns. Will your bins piled high with straw and fresh manure be visible from your neighbors' patio, where they sit and watch birds? Also, check homeowner association or other municipal regulations that may influence your options.

Choosing a convenient site

The ideal location for composting is within easy reach of a hose. You'll apply water to each pile as you build, uniformly moistening all the organic matter. And if you decide to regularly turn and maintain your compost, you'll be remoistening piles again and again. A gallon of water weighs over 8 pounds, so it's unlikely you'll want to lug sufficient water to keep your compost bins churning out a finished product!

If you have a large property and compost on the outskirts, rather than dragging a hose, consider extending your underground water line and installing a hose bib close to the action.

How much space you need depends on the ultimate scope of your composting operation and what style of bins, if any, you decide to use. (Chapter 5 helps you envision bin shapes and sizes.) At its most basic, a freestanding pile of organic matter (without a bin enclosing it) should be *at least* 3 feet long x 3 feet wide x 3 feet tall (1 meter long x 1 meter wide x 1 meter tall) — up to 5 x 5 x 5 feet (1.5 x 1.5 x 1.5 meters), as depicted in Figure 8-1. (See the later section "Finding the pile size that's just right" for more size considerations.) Don't forget to allow yourself elbow room to comfortably swing a pitchfork loaded with organic matter and shovel your finished compost into a bucket, wheelbarrow, or cart for transport elsewhere in the landscape.

Ideal pile size: 3–5 cubic (1–1.5 cubic meters)

Figure 8-1: The optimal size for a freestanding pile is 3 to 5 cubic feet (1 to 1.5 cubic meters).

However, don't let lack of space deter you from composting. Even the smallest courtyard garden or balcony has a corner for a compact compost bin design or a worm bin (see Chapter 10 for more on this), and good-looking bin designs are available for those who have nowhere to hide their composting efforts.

Because finished compost is heavy, setting up close to where the finished compost will be used makes sense. If you plan to add garden beds or planting areas in the future, compost right on top of those spots. Your composting effort will somewhat soften the top layer of soil beneath it, making it easier to dig, and nutrients leached from the compost pile will give a boost to new plants. Compost directly on the ground (not on concrete or other hardscape surfaces) to promote good contact with soil microorganisms, aeration, and drainage.

As for other practical considerations for locating your compost area, think about whether you plan to add fresh organic matter frequently and whether you want to turn the organic matter. If you don't regularly turn, water, or monitor a pile, it may be fine to locate it out of sight, out of mind, in the far corner of your yard behind a hedge or garden shed, decomposing slowly over time. Alternatively, if you want to recycle all your kitchen waste daily, adding scraps frequently is easier when the pile is close at hand.

Climate considerations

Regardless of where you live, site your compost area in the shade if at all possible. Shade keeps the organic matter from drying out rapidly. (It also keeps you from dehydrating in the sun when the time comes to toss a ton of organic matter.)

Wet compost turns stinky fast and is heavy to turn. If you live in a rainy climate, avoid places beneath eaves where downpours leach nutrients and create a soggy mess. Also avoid areas with poor drainage where rainwater puddles, forcing you to slog through mud.

If you share property with mosquitoes or those equally nasty biting horseflies, tending a compost area at the far edge of a property seems unbearable. If you want to keep your compost cooking through the year while avoiding biters, consider an enclosed bin near the back door for kitchen scraps, so you can dash in and out quickly.

Cold and snowy winters don't have to stop you from adding ingredients to your pile. If you want to add kitchen scraps or other materials through the winter, situate the compost area where you can reach it easily — unless you like to strap on snowshoes and get exercise, of course! (Check out Chapter 5 for more ideas on what to do with kitchen waste.)

Creating Your Pile

At last, you're ready to start piling up the goods. This section explains how you can speed decomposition by creating a pile of optimum proportions and prepping ingredients before tossing them on the heap. It also covers methods for enhancing airflow that you build into the pile while layering and moistening the composting ingredients.

Finding the pile size that's just right

For a typical backyard situation, a freestanding pile that is 3 x 3 x 3 feet (1 cubic yard or 1 cubic meter) is both easily managed and efficient. It provides sufficient bulk for the organic matter to self-insulate, creating a moist, warm interior for all the microbes to live and reproduce in while maintaining the heat that their activity generates. (Chapter 3 covers compost critters in detail.)

A pile that's 1 cubic yard in size can heat up sufficiently to kill most weed seeds and plant pathogens, but only if you maintain it properly. You must create a specific pile type and maintain it rigorously in order to kill weed seeds and plant diseases — the section "Compost for Type-A personalities" later in this chapter provides step-by-step instructions for this type of pile.

If you have the space and materials, you can start out by creating a larger pile, up to 4 or even 5 cubic feet (1.2 to 1.5 cubic meters), as shown in Figure 8-1. However, going larger than 5 cubic feet (1.5 cubic meters) doesn't allow sufficient air circulation through the center of the pile, and the decomposition process slows. Plus, turning a bigger pile is more cumbersome. If you want to try your hand at large-scale composting, turn to Chapter 4.

To chop or not to chop: Adding small or large chunks

The smaller the pieces of organic matter in your compost, the faster the rate of decomposition.

Lots and lots of small pieces offer more surface area for micro-organisms and macroorganisms to chomp on. It's analogous to cooking up a stir-fry meal. If you slice and dice the veggies into bite-size pieces before tossing them into a wok, they cook faster, and you can enjoy dinner much sooner than if you throw a whole onion and head of cabbage into the pan.

Chop, break, and shred most of the material into small pieces. There doesn't have to be anything tidy or uniform about it. Your goal is to offer as many entry wounds as possible for critters to attack. Incorporate these routines into your garden cleanup:

- ✔ **Break thin branches over your knee or cut them into smaller pieces with hand pruners and loppers as you prune.**

- ✔ **Chop weeds with a hoe or square-bladed spade.**

- ✔ **Tear apart spent annuals as you pull them from the garden with your gloved hands.**

- ✔ **Set aside an area for chopping refuse with a hatchet or machete (an excellent stress reducer, by the way).** Use smooth, flat ground surface or a large tree stump. Wear protective safety glasses when chopping.

- ✔ **Consider renting or buying a chipper/shredder if you have lots of woody material to deal with.**

Although most of your compost material should be small pieces, it's okay — even beneficial — to allow some bulk to remain to provide air pockets. If all the contents of your pile are tiny, compacted bits (such as grass clippings, shredded leaves, wet manure, sawdust), they compress and form impenetrable mats, reducing the ability of oxygen to circulate through the pile. Composting critters need oxygen to thrive, and if the oxygen in the pile is depleted, they die without reproducing in sufficient numbers to keep the process moving steadily along. Avoid this problem by incorporating a variety of material sizes. Mix the small materials well or spread them in ultra-thin layers — never thick, impenetrable layers. Aim to achieve a mix of "greens" (moist materials) and "browns" (dry ones), and you can't go wrong!

Aerating made easy

In aerobic composting, oxygen is needed for decomposition. (Chapter 4 covers aerobic composting in more detail.) Decomposing organisms use up initial air supplies quickly. Without sufficient oxygen to fuel the composting organisms (as I describe in Chapter 3), the process slows. Decomposition won't screech to a complete halt, but it will definitely slacken. Turning the pile periodically to add more oxygen kicks it back into gear, as I explain in the later section, "Tending to the Compost Pile."

If you don't want to turn your pile frequently (or at all), don't worry. Compost will still make itself, it'll just take longer. However, it'll help if you incorporate one or more of the following methods to promote aeration as you construct your pile:

✔ **Start with a layer of larger, woody branch trimmings, dead perennial stems, or cornstalks at the bottom of the pile (this lets in lots of air from the base), and scatter some throughout the pile as you build it.** This makes it a bit more difficult to turn the pile because large, woody chunks get stuck in fork tines.

✔ **Lay a wooden shipping pallet down as the foundation of your compost pile.** (If you garden where soil drainage is poor, do this in addition to incorporating trimmings as noted in the preceding bullet; otherwise, one or the other is sufficient.) The pallet sits a few inches aboveground, allowing air circulation beneath. Try this if achieving sufficient aeration is a problem because the ground remains damp or it rains a lot.

✔ **Insert one or more airflow tubes into the midst of the pile during construction, adding material around them as you build, as shown in Figure 8-2.** Make tubes from leftover lengths of PVC (polyvinyl chloride) drainpipe (any diameter over 2 inches [5 centimeters] is good), chicken wire, or hardware cloth. Drill holes into PVC pipe every 6 inches (15 centimeters) or so along the length of the pipe. Or, roll chicken wire or hardware cloth into a cylindrical shape. Tubes should be long enough to reach the bottom of the pile and extend to the top of the bin. Airflow tubes serve double-duty because they can also be used to add water to the pile's interior if it dries out.

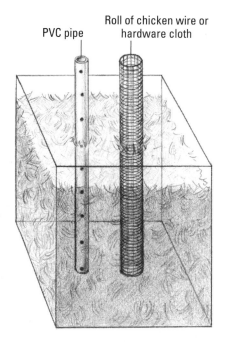

PVC pipe

Roll of chicken wire or hardware cloth

Figure 8-2: Airflow tubes allow airflow through the pile to aid the decomposition process.

Piling on the layers — and watering as you work

Do you prefer chocolate layer cake or tossed salad? When it comes to constructing a compost pile, you can alternate layers of browns and greens like a chocolate layer cake (with green frosting), or toss everything together like a giant chopped salad. (Turn to Chapter 7 for an explanation of brown and green compost ingredients.) Generally, the more mixed up the ingredients, the better the overall decomposition, because different ingredient layers can decompose at different rates. But layering is usually easier for most folks, plus you can add layers to the pile as more ingredients become available. Layer your pile as follows, starting at the bottom:

1. **4 inches (10 centimeters) of chunky browns (sticks, woody trimmings, dried perennial stems, cornstalks, and the like) to promote aeration at the bottom**

2. **4 to 5 inches (10 to 13 centimeters) of other browns (leaves, straw, woody trimmings, paper products, pine needles, sawdust)**

3. **2 to 3 inches (5 to 8 centimeters) of greens (kitchen scraps, grass clippings, leafy plant trimmings, manure)**

4. **Repeat Steps 2 and 3 until you reach a pile height of 3 to 5 feet. Finish with a top layer of browns to insulate.**

As I mention in the earlier section "To chop or not to chop: Adding small or large chunks," if you have small, compact materials, such as grass clippings, sawdust, or wet manure, mix them in small quantities with other materials, or use them in ultra-thin layers.

Whether you layer or mix your compost pile isn't really that big of a deal. The more important issue is to ensure that all your recipe ingredients are sufficiently moist as you build. Just like humans, decomposing microorganisms need moisture to thrive. If the organic materials in your compost pile dry out — or if they're too dry to begin with — the composting process is derailed. Organic materials — especially the carbons, such as sawdust, dried leaves, or shredded paper — require you to add water as you build your pile.

If you wait to moisten the entire compost pile from the top after you construct it, the water will quickly find the path of least resistance to the ground, forming a puddle at the base while bypassing the majority of the organic matter. Instead, use a hose with an on/off spray attachment, and sprinkle each layer (or every 10 to 12 shovel- or pitchfork-loads) of organic matter as you build. Everything should have the moisture level of a wrung-out sponge, so grab a handful every once in a while as you build, and test it.

Tending to the Compost Pile

A well-constructed pile can be left to rot on its own timetable, rewarding you with useable compost in three to six months. If you want to dig out black gold faster than that, or if you didn't have quite the right mix of ingredients on hand when you created your pile, you can speed the process by turning and remoistening the pile and incorporating more ingredients as needed.

Table 8-1 touches on some possible problems you may encounter when tending to your compost pile. For more-detailed troubleshooting information, turn to Chapter 14.

Table 8-1		What's Wrong with My Compost Pile?
Problem	**Cause**	**Solution**
Slow decomposition	Lack of nitrogen	Add "green" nitrogen-rich organic matter (see Chapter 7).
Slow decomposition	Poor aeration	Turn pile.
Slow decomposition	Too dry	Turn pile and remoisten all materials.
Slow decomposition	Pile too small	Add more organic matter to increase pile size to 3–5 cubic feet (1–1.5 cubic meters).
Slow decomposition	Cold weather	Insulate outer pile with thick layers of cardboard, sod, straw, or leaves. Use a compost bin style with a lid to retain heat. Increase pile size.
Ammonia odor	Too much nitrogen	Add "brown" carbon-rich materials and remix (see Chapter 7).
Rotten odor	Too wet	Add "brown" carbon-rich materials and remix (see Chapter 7).
Attracts flies	Kitchen scraps too close to top of pile	Bury scraps in center of pile. Don't add meats, dairy, oils, or grease.
Attracts dogs, raccoons, or other pests	Kitchen scraps too close to top of pile	Bury scraps in center of pile. Don't add meats, dairy, oils, or grease. Use an animal-proof enclosed bin.
White or gray thread-like filaments resembling spider webs on the outer edges of the pile	Actinomycetes, a type of bacteria, are at work decomposing organic matter	No change required. These are "good guys" (see Chapter 3).
Contains grubs, worms, and other large bugs	No worries! Indicates nature is at work.	No change required.

Turning your compost pile

Just a few days after creation, your towering mountain of compost will shrink noticeably. This is exactly what should be happening. The decomposers are using up oxygen, collapsing millions of tiny air spaces between all those bits of organic matter. Without oxygen, the decomposing population drops, and the decomposition process slows. To keep the process rolling — or if your goal is to cook up a hot pile to kill weed seeds — you must introduce a fresh oxygen supply by turning the organic matter. (See "Compost for Type-A personalities" later in this chapter for guidelines on creating and sustaining a hot pile.)

To turn a freestanding pile, simply fork the material into a new heap adjacent to the original one, remoistening as needed (see the next section for watering instructions). If you have only one container, fork out the material onto the ground and then back in, mixing as you go. The easiest option is to have an empty bin available so you can simply transfer your compost from one bin to another. Some bin styles and configurations are more labor-saving than others when it comes to turning frequently, such as tumblers; Chapter 5 describes those options in detail.

Turning the entire pile is the most effective aeration method. But if you can't do that regularly, another option is to plunge an aerating tool in the midst of the organic matter. Chapter 2 explains how these tools work and covers the pros and cons of different styles. Aerating tools don't introduce as much oxygen as completely overturning the entire pile, but they churn things up somewhat. Within the confines of smaller bins, aerating tools are usually easier to maneuver than shovels or forks when turning material.

Adding water

As you turn your pile, have the hose ready to sprinkle the material with water as you work. All the organic matter should be moist like a wrung-out sponge — just like it was when you constructed the pile — so grab a few handfuls of the material as you're turning it to check the moisture level. And just as in the initial construction, if you try to remoisten the entire compost pile from the top, most of the water will end up in a puddle at your feet.

If you're not going to turn but still need to moisten, sprinkle in small increments over a period of time, allowing the water to penetrate through the pile. Also, if rain is predicted when your compost is dry, remove any tarps, lids, or covers to take advantage of the free water.

When Is It Finished — And Why Does It Matter?

Ready-to-use compost resembles rich, dark, crumbly soil. Particles are fairly uniform in size, and you shouldn't be able to recognize the original ingredients. (However, in a home composting endeavor, it's not unusual to spy larger chunks of undecomposed materials, such as woody stems or clumps of matted leaves. Simply toss this material back into your compost area to break down further in the next batch.) Your compost pile should no longer be generating significant heat and should have reduced in size by one-third to one-half. Finished compost emits a pleasant, earthy aroma. Squeeze a handful of compost. It should feel moist, but it shouldn't be so wet that it's squishy, nor so dry that it blows away like pro-verbial dust in the wind.

Try to restrain from raiding the compost pile until it's finished. No matter how you're using organic matter in your garden or landscape, finished compost is easier to work with than lumpy material full of corncobs, sticks, and pinecones. Nutrients in well-decomposed organic matter are ready for plants to use. Finished compost's deep color and fine texture makes attractive mulch when spread around plants or on top of containers (see Chapter 9). Most importantly, well-decomposed organic matter is safer for your plants.

If you incorporate uncomposted or partially decomposed organic matter into a garden shortly before planting, soil microorganisms continue to break the matter down, effectively competing with your young seedlings or plants for nutrients. Such microbial activity ties up available nitrogen in the soil in a process called *nitrogen immobilization*. Because nitrogen is one of three essential nutrients (phosphorus and potassium are the others) for healthy plant development, your flowers and vegetables may exhibit signs of stunted growth or yellowing. Organic acids in undecomposed materials may also harm plant roots. If you want to plant soon, improve the soil in gardens only with finished compost. Another option is to spread uncomposted matter but wait to plant. How long to wait depends on the organic matter and how much decom-position still needs to take place. Figure from at least one month up to as long as one year for fresh manure.

Chapter 9 gives you in-depth information about where and how to use your finished compost in your gardens and landscaping.

Surveying Different Approaches to Making Compost

Composting is a great activity, in part because it's so adaptable: Compost strategies exist to address all needs, schedules, and personality types! This section provides instructions for a number of methods that run the gamut from very little work to regular monitoring.

Basic compost for laid-back gardeners

This easy recipe for a freestanding pile works well for just about anyone. You can also follow these instructions but layer the material in a bin of some sort, if you choose to use a compost container. (I describe bins in Chapter 5.) As you gain experience, these steps serve as a starting point for developing your own favorite composting formula:

1. **Spread 4 inches (10 centimeters) of chunkier, dry, brown materials — such as branch trimmings, corn stalks, or straw — as the base to promote good aeration.**

   If unavailable, use other browns you have on hand and insert an airflow tube as described in the earlier section "Aerating made easy." (See Chapter 7 for other possible ingredients.)

   Sprinkle all materials with water as you build. Organic matter should have the moisture of a wrung-out sponge.

2. **Layer 4 to 5 inches (10 to 13 centimeters) of additional brown materials, such as dry leaves or shredded paper.**

   Moisten all materials as you work.

3. **Toss in a few handfuls (or shovelfuls) of your native soil between layers as you build.**

   It's loaded with microorganisms ready to work.

4. **Layer 2 to 3 inches (5 to 8 centimeters) of green materials — such as grass clippings, kitchen scraps, spent garden annuals, or manure — on top of the browns.**

   Moisten all materials as you work.

5. **Continue alternating and moistening layers of browns and greens, ending with a layer of browns on top to insulate the pile.**

   Your final pile should be a minimum of 3 cubic feet (1 cubic yard or 1 cubic meter), up to a maximum of 5 cubic feet (1.5 cubic meters). Refer to Figure 8-1.

6. **Optional: Cover the pile with a tarp.**

   In rainy locales, the tarp prevents the pile from getting too soggy. In arid regions, it prevents material from drying out.

If you do nothing further at this point, you'll have some harvestable compost from the bottom and center of the pile in three to six months. Variations occur based on how small the pieces of organic matter are at the start and how long the pile retains moisture and aeration in your region.

Toss any chunks of organic material that don't decompose fully the first time around (especially from the outside edges of the pile) into the next pile you construct.

 If you turn and remoisten basic compost once or twice, you'll have more compost sooner (refer to the earlier section "Tending to the Compost Pile"). If you enjoy turning the pile, you may want to start out with the recipe for speedier compost in the next section.

Speedier compost

This method requires more upfront labor chopping or shredding the organic matter, as well as regular turning of the pile. But you'll be able to harvest more compost in a shorter time frame.

1. **Follow the recipe for basic compost in the previous section, but chop or shred all materials into small pieces before layering.**

   After several days, the pile will shrink noticeably in size.

2. **Turn the entire pile, making sure materials on the outer edges get mixed into the interior to promote even decomposition.**

   Remoisten if needed.

3. **If you're gung-ho, after a week or two, turn and remoisten the pile.**

   If you're less than gung-ho and don't want to perform any labor that isn't absolutely essential, dig into the center of the pile with your pitchfork and check to see whether it's warm and moist. If so, you can skip turning. If it feels dry or cool, it needs turning and watering.

4. **Repeat the process every two or three weeks.**

   Check the organic matter for heat and moisture, and turn and moisten it as needed.

After three or four turnings, you'll have harvestable compost.

Compost for Type-A personalities

If you want compost in a hurry, a hot pile suits your style. *Hot piles* are just that: They heat up to temperatures of 120 to 170 degrees Fahrenheit (49 to 77 degrees Celsius) within 1 to 5 days, with 150 degrees Fahrenheit (66 degrees Celsius) being a typical peak. Your role is to help the pile maintain high temperatures by monitoring it with a thermometer and turning all the material when the temperature cools. Also, you want to make sure the pile doesn't get too hot (staying above 150 degrees Fahrenheit [66 degrees Celsius] for more than a few hours), because that much heat will kill beneficial microorganisms that add value to your composting process.

A well-constructed and properly managed hot pile will turn organic matter into compost within four weeks.

Hot piles have a few drawbacks:

- ✔ They're labor-intensive, requiring regular monitoring and turning four times within one month.
- ✔ The carbon to nitrogen ratio of the ingredients is less forgiving than that of other composting methods. (See Chapter 7 for information on ingredients and C:N ratios.)
- ✔ All ingredients must be available at the outset to construct the pile.
- ✔ The ingredients must be chopped small and fine.
- ✔ The moisture level must be maintained.
- ✔ Microorganisms use up nitrogen to fuel this fast process, so finished compost may be lower in nitrogen content than that produced by other active composting methods.

Hot piles have a couple advantages, too:

✔ Compost is available for use faster via this method than other methods.

✔ The process kills most weed seeds and plant pathogens, allowing you to recycle more organic matter onsite to keep it out of the waste stream. (See the sidebar "Killer compost" for details.)

✔ Maintaining a hot pile is great exercise! You'll save a fortune on gym membership by turning your compost regularly as you work on hot composting.

To get started on your quick-decomposing piles, gather these materials:

✔ Equal parts green and brown materials, all shredded to a small size. Fresh grass clippings and dried shredded leaves work great for your first effort because they're already in small pieces, and the grass clippings are full of moisture. However, you can use any of the greens and browns described in Chapter 7, as long as you chop them into bits.

✔ A fork and/or shovel for turning.

✔ A compost thermometer. (If you don't have a compost thermometer, attach a meat thermometer to the end of a stick.)

✔ A tarp (optional).

✔ A bin (optional).

When you have everything you need to get started, follow these steps:

1. **Chop or shred organic matter into small pieces.**

2. **Toss the greens and browns together in a well-blended mix (not layers).**

3. **Add a shovelful of already finished compost or native soil, which will be full of microorganisms to jumpstart the process.**

    Sprinkle water as you build, moistening all the organic matter to the consistency of a wrung-out sponge.

    Your final pile must be at least 3 cubic feet (1 cubic meter) in size and no more than 5 cubic feet (1.5 cubic meters) to help maintain sufficient heat and moisture to speed decomposition.

4. **Optional: Cover with a burlap or other breathable tarp to maintain moisture.**

5. **Monitor and record your pile's daily temperature with a compost thermometer.**

   Temperatures will rise to 120 to 170 degrees Fahrenheit (49 to 77 degrees Celsius), usually within one to five days.

   Temperature trends are approximate and vary depending on the type of materials you're composting, the size of the pieces, the level of moisture, and so on. Monitor the trend of rising and dropping temperatures, but don't worry about achieving exact readings unless you need to kill weed seeds or plant pathogens in the pile. If that's your goal, check out the nearby sidebar, "Killer compost."

6. **Every four to seven days, when the temperature of the pile cools below 110 degrees Fahrenheit (43 degrees Celsius), turn all of the organic matter to introduce more oxygen and heat it back up.**

   Thoroughly mix materials from the pile's exterior to the interior. If needed, water as you turn to maintain the wrung-out-sponge moisture level. Be careful not to get material too wet, because doing so cools off the pile.

7. **After about 14 days, the ingredients of the organic matter will no longer be recognizable. Continue monitoring and recording daily temperatures, and repeating the turning process.**

   Turn every four to five days, when the temperature drops below 110 degrees Fahrenheit (43 degrees Celsius). Remoisten if needed. Turn a total of four times throughout one month.

8. **After 1 month, the pile no longer heats up after turning, and the bulk of it is dark, crumbly compost.**

   The temperature drops to 85 degrees Fahrenheit (29 degrees Celsius) or lower.

9. **At this point, let the compost "cure" for one to two weeks before spreading around plants or adding to gardens for planting.**

Killer compost

As a practical matter, most backyard composting efforts don't heat up sufficiently to kill weed seeds and pathogens. I've experimented with hot piles at my cooperative extension demonstration site. It's fun and a good learning experience, but also time-consuming. If you're uncertain about your ability to maintain a hot pile, it's better to be safe than sorry and dispose of all weed seeds or diseased plant material in the trash. You can still have a blast experimenting with hot batches without worrying whether the bad stuff might end up back in your garden.

If you're still gung-ho to try after that warning, it's essential to monitor pile temperatures to ensure they stay hot enough long enough to do the job, without heating up so much that they wipe out beneficial microorganisms and shut down your composting process.

Different temperature levels and time periods are required to kill different weeds seeds and pathogens. Follow the instructions in "Compost for Type-A personalities," with these add-ons:

✔ Most plants diseases are neutralized if temperatures stay between 130 and 140 degrees Fahrenheit (54 to 60 degrees Celsius) for 72 hours.

✔ Most weed seeds are killed if exposed to temperatures above 131 degrees Fahrenheit (55 degrees Celsius) for 72 hours.

✔ Turn the pile multiple times to ensure that all materials on the exterior receive their "cooking time" on the interior. The pile must reheat to the appropriate range for three days each time you turn it.

A fine three-bin compost

The three-bin method allows your compost to age gracefully or be ready in a hurry, whatever your needs. It's a great labor-saving system if you have space for three adjacent bins, as shown in Chapter 6. It's also an efficient method for stockpiling and processing large quantities of organic materials.

1. Load Bin 1 with organic material to start decomposing.

Follow the earlier instructions for basic compost to get started, or use your favorite compost recipe.

2. **When the materials are ready to be turned, pitchfork the contents into Bin 2, remoistening everything as you work.**

   They're usually ready within four to six weeks, but you can speed up or slow down the cycle to suit your needs.

3. **Leave any large chunks of organic matter that haven't broken down sufficiently in Bin 1, where you'll begin adding more fresh carbon- and nitrogen-rich materials to start a new pile.**

4. **When the contents of Bin 2 become unrecognizable (usually in another four to six weeks), turn the contents into Bin 3 to decompose further into finished compost.**

   Bin 3 also serves as a handy holding bin until you're ready to use your compost.

5. **Continue the cycle, rotating material from Bins 1 to 2 to 3.**

Compost smoothie, anyone?

Some gardeners enjoy putting their kitchen scraps in a blender with a little water, whipping them into an unappetizing slurry, and then pouring the mixture into the compost pile or into holes dug in the garden. If this appeals to you, go for it. (Bury the slurry within the pile or ground to reduce potential odors or pests.)

Chapter 9

Using Your Finished Compost

*W*hether you make it or buy it, compost is a multitasking miracle worker. It doesn't matter whether you're a first-time gardener or an established green thumb maintaining a landscape that your neighbors covet: You're sure to benefit from at least one of compost's many uses.

This chapter tells you how to put finished compost to work for your plants, including instructions for screening compost for use in certain applications. You also get recommendations on supplementing your homemade compost with store-bought compost if you find that your supply is running a bit low.

Enriching Vegetable and Flower Beds

A healthy garden starts with healthy soil. You don't need to worry about applying miracle elixirs or wielding new-fangled tools. Adding compost to garden beds is the best — and easiest — thing you can do to produce a bumper crop of vegetables and bountiful bouquets of flowers. Reread that sentence and commit it to memory!

In clay soils, compost enhances drainage; in sandy soils, it increases water retention. No matter what your soil type, compost adds nutrients and improves *tilth,* which refers to soil's overall structure and workability. Compost aerates the soil, encourages all sorts of beneficial microbial activity, and serves as a beacon to attract earthworms, Mother Nature's soil-building contractors. The only negative I can think of to applying compost to the garden is that it isn't a one-time event!

How much compost you need to apply and how often you should apply it varies, depending on the typical soil characteristics and whether you garden year-round. The following sections dig into these details.

Knowing how often to add compost to garden beds

New gardeners are sometimes surprised by how quickly the thick layer of compost they dug into their garden seems to have disappeared. As Chapter 3 describes, an army of soil organisms is working diligently to reduce organic matter to ever-smaller constituent parts.

As a general rule, plan on incorporating compost into your beds before each planting season.

When your planting season occurs and how many planting seasons you get each calendar year depends on geography.

One-season gardens

Apply compost once per year if you live in cooler climes, such as the Northeast or Midwest United States, Canada, or the United Kingdom, where there's one major growing season — from late spring to early fall.

Layer partially decomposed compost on empty beds in fall before the ground freezes and let it decompose further through winter. All those lovely nutrients will be ready and waiting for your spring planting.

Alternatively, being cooped up inside wearing winter woolens while perusing seed catalogs may leave you a little stir crazy for some gardening activity come spring. It's okay to incorporate compost in early spring rather than fall, but use finished compost, so nutrients are readily available for your plants.

Year-round gardens

If you live in the South or Southwest United States, where a warm climate offers year-round gardening, you need to add compost twice per year to accommodate two distinct growing seasons — one cool and one warm — with different annual flowers, vegetables, and herbs planted and thriving in each period.

Because the ground never freezes in warmer climates, soil microbes are working year-round, plowing through organic matter faster than their cool-country cousins. Also, some warm-climate gardeners work with native soils that are naturally low in organic matter.

Here's a general schedule for applying compost where year-round gardening is possible:

- ✔ **Cool season:** The cool growing season extends from approximately mid September through April, so add compost in late August or early September.

- ✔ **Warm season:** Warm-season planting (which overlaps with the ongoing cool-season growth period), starts about mid to late February and runs through March, with warm season plants continuing to grow though summer. Add finished compost before your area's spring planting season.

  Alternatively, if your garden lies empty during intense summer heat, spread compost and let it cover the fallow soil to reduce erosion, combat weeds, and maintain moisture.

For advice on soil improvement and optimum planting dates in your area, contact your county cooperative extension office in the United States. Every state has extension offices serving as the public outreach arm of the state's land grant university. Some offices also offer Master Gardener programs with trained volunteers to answer gardening questions. Find your county office by searching online under "cooperative extension" and your state name. Or, look in the white pages' county government listings for "cooperative extension" or the name of your state's land grant university, such as "University of Arizona Cooperative Extension" or "Iowa State University Extension." In Canada, Master Gardener programs are affiliated with a variety of organizations, including universities and public gardens. Find Master Gardeners near you with an Internet search.

Figuring out how much compost is enough on beds

If you're starting a new garden bed, first determine whether the soil is organically rich. This doesn't have to be an exact science, so you can use a simple "eyeball test" — light-colored soil doesn't contain as much organic matter as dark brown or black soil. Then follow these guidelines:

✔ **Soil with limited organic matter:** Where soil isn't organically rich, add 4 to 6 inches (10 to 15 centimeters) of compost before each planting season.

✔ **Soil with plentiful organic matter:** If you garden where soil is organically rich, 1 to 3 inches (3 to 7 centimeters) of fresh compost will suffice before each season.

The root systems of most annual flowers and vegetables remain within the top 12 inches (30 centimeters) of soil. Loosening up your soil to that depth helps roots penetrate freely to seek moisture and nutrients. Follow these recommendations for loosening soil and digging in compost:

✔ If you're lucky to garden where soil is already loose, easy to dig in, and drains readily, you can layer compost on top of the soil and dig it in to a depth of 6 to 12 inches (15 to 30 centimeters) in one step.

✔ If soil is compacted, drainage is poor, or you garden above a layer of *hardpan* (impenetrable subsoil that restricts water movement and root growth), you'll grow a more successful garden if you first dig and loosen soil to a depth of 12 inches (30 centimeters). Then layer your compost on top of the soil and turn it under to a depth of 6 to 12 inches (15 to 30 centimeters).

Over time, with continued compost additions, your garden soil will transform into a richer, earthier concoction than what you started with. How much you put on each year can vary — you be the judge: Were your plants healthy and productive without it? Does the soil retain moisture? Do plenty of earthworms tunnel about? If you answer "yes" to these questions, you can cut back on your compost applications.

Using Compost to Mulch Landscape Plants and Trees

Mulch is any substance spread on top of the soil to maintain consistent soil moisture, inhibit weed seed germination and growth, and moderate soil temperatures. In hot climates, mulch keeps root zones cooler; in cold climates, a layer of mulch in winter helps insulate roots and reduces *frost heave* — ground upheaval caused by freezing and thawing of moist soil, which negatively impacts root systems.

Luckily for you, compost makes tremendous mulch. Organic mulch, such as that derived from compost, has all the usual benefits in addition to supplying nutrients to the soil as it decomposes. On beds of permanent plants, trees, hedges, and fruit, an annual mulch of compost will keep your soil in good health and your plants in top condition.

Here are a few more advantages of compost mulch:

- ✓ Compost's rich, dark color and crumbly uniform texture adds an attractive, "finished" look to planting areas.

- ✓ Compost mulch breaks down faster than bark chips or shredded wood chips, releasing its nutrients more quickly for plants to absorb. Keep in mind that because compost mulch breaks down faster, it needs to be reapplied more frequently than wood-chip mulch, perhaps yearly.

- ✓ Compost mulch doesn't harbor artillery fungi *(Sphaerobolus stellatus)* or other nuisance fungi found in some regional wood-chip mulches. Reproduction efforts of these so-called "shotgun" fungi involve shooting messy black or brown spores through the air, which are difficult to clean off buildings, cars, and patio surfaces.

- ✓ Birds and other wildlife are delighted by compost-rich beds that are also rich in worms and other creatures on which to feast.

Keep weed seeds out of your composting efforts so they don't live to sprout around your landscape after you spread compost mulch. (See Chapter 6 for details on weed-free composting.)

Figure 9-1 shows where to spread compost mulch — around the base of a plant outwards to the canopy edge, always keeping it away from the stem or trunk because wet mulch in contact with plant tissue creates a hospitable environment for disease and pest problems. Keep pace with expanding canopies by adding more compost mulch as plants grow.

How thick a layer of compost mulch you need to apply varies, depending on climate and soil conditions. If you're an arid-land gardener, apply 2 to 4 inches (5 to 10 centimeters) around plants. If you garden in cool climes, 2 to 3 inches (5 to 8 centimeters) is sufficient.

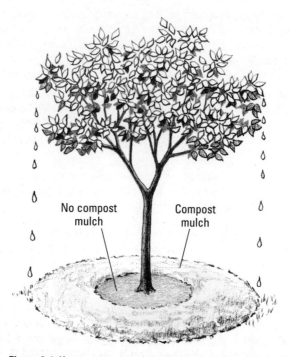

Figure 9-1: Keep compost mulch 4 to 6 inches (10 to 15 centimeters) away from stems and trunks.

Although it was once standard practice to amend a tree or shrub's planting hole backfill with compost or other organic matter, this is no longer recommended. For a landscape plant to develop, its roots must spread outwards into native surrounding soil to access water and nutrients and to develop a strong anchor. Researchers discovered that roots tend to stay cozily ensconced within amended planting holes. The plants effectively become rootbound, as if they were still confined to their nursery pot. However, if you are filling a border with mixed plants, dig and enrich the entire bed with compost before planting.

Top-Dressing Lawns

Top-dressing is applying a light scattering of compost, other mulch, or sometimes fertilizer, over soil surfaces to add organic matter or nutrients without digging it in. You can use compost to top-dress both new and existing lawns.

> ✔ **On a seeded lawn:** After sowing lawn grass seeds, apply a thin layer — about ¼-inch (6 millimeters) — of compost as

top-dressing to help maintain consistent soil moisture while seeds germinate and tender grass seedlings get established. Top-dressing is especially helpful in arid climates or during dry or breezy spells, where the soil and seeds easily dry out within hours. (If a germinated seed dries out, it's a goner.)

✔ **On an existing lawn:** Top-dressing with compost may also rejuvenate existing lawns. Lawns often become compacted over time from foot traffic, play, and mowing, which prevents air, water, and nutrients from circulating freely through the turf's root zone.

Top-dressing is more effective if the turf is *core aerated* before spreading the compost. Basically, core aerating involves poking small holes in the top few inches of lawn to encourage the flow of air, water, and nutrients. To core aerate a small patch of turf, use a specialized foot press that you can find at your local home and garden store. For large lawns, rent a machine from an equipment supply company or hire a lawn maintenance firm.

When top-dressing with compost, you should only use screened compost (I explain screening in the next section) or compost with particle sizes of ⅜-inch or less. Small compost particles infiltrate between blades of grass more easily than large particles, which may smother the grass. Also, take care to top-dress with compost that's guaranteed free of weed seeds, or you may be sowing a future weeding nightmare into your lawn!

No matter where you live, the best time to aerate and top-dress your lawn is when it is most actively growing. This allows the grass to vigorously rebound after having holes punched in it.

If you live in either a cool or "transition" climate and grow one permanent turfgrass (such as bluegrass or fescue), the best time to aerate your lawn is spring to mid-summer. Avoid aerating these grasses during summer's intense heat, which may stress roots. Although some growth occurs in early fall, these types of grasses go semi- or fully dormant as weather cools, making recovery after a late aeration more stressful. Also, early aeration promotes better penetration of summer and fall rains through the soil when it's most beneficial for growth. Improved soil penetration with rainfall creates a healthier, stronger lawn that has a better chance of making it through harsh winters unscathed.

If you live in a warm climate that allows year-round lawns, you have different options. The best time to aerate and top-dress is early to mid-summer when your warm-season lawn (such as Bermuda grass) is actively growing. You should also apply compost top-dressing (without aeration) after overseeding your summer lawn with a cool-season grass (such as ryegrass) in the fall. If you don't overseed, there's no need to top-dress in fall.

Irrigate immediately after top-dressing (unless rain does the job for you). Water disperses the compost evenly amongst the grass blades.

Screening Compost for Containers

Screening compost is simply pushing compost back and forth over a wire screen to remove pinecones, twigs, and other chunks of undecomposed material. Screening leaves you with only the finest, lightweight compost, with more air pockets than compressed garden soil. It also removes the larger seeds that survive composting and would be happy to sprout in undesirable places.

This section explains how easy it is to make and use a compost screen, and gives tips on using screened compost.

Making a compost screen

If you're all thumbs when it comes to hammers and nails, you can buy a compost screen from garden supply catalogs. Also search the Internet using terms such as "soil screen" or "soil sifter." Some manufactured compost bins come with screening attachments.

If you're the do-it-yourself type, gather the following materials to make your own screen:

- **Hardware cloth:** This stiff, galvanized wire screen with small openings is available at hardware stores and home improvement centers. The ½-inch size (1 centimeter) works well for compost screening; ¼-inch (0.5 centimeter) will produce finer results.

- **Scrap lumber:** Scrap lumber is used to make a frame to hold the wire. The optimal size depends on your preference and the receptacle you plan to hold the screen over, such as a bucket, wheelbarrow, garden cart, or bin. Typical wood sizes for screens are 1 x 2s, 1 x 3s, or 2 x 2s.

You may think: "Aha! A giant frame will allow me to produce enormous quantities of screened compost faster than my neighbor." Keep in mind, though, that compost, like soil, is heavy, so take your lower back into account! A frame that is 18 to 24 inches (45 to 60 centimeters) square is easy to manage for most gardeners.

✔ **Saw:** If you're purchasing lumber and are tool challenged, some home centers may cut the wood for you.

✔ **Wire cutter or tin snips:** Use these to cut hardware cloth.

✔ **Heavy-duty stapler:** You use this to affix the wire to the frame.

After you have your materials, follow these simple steps to construct the screen in Figure 9-2:

1. **Cut the lumber to your desired size, and nail the ends together. Make a second frame of the same size.**

2. **Cut the wire, allowing about 1 inch (2.5 centimeters) extra to overlap all four sides of the frame for attachment.**

3. **Stretch the wire tightly across the frame, and staple it securely to each side of the frame.**

4. **Lay the second frame over the stapled edges of the screen, and nail it to the first frame for a secure and long-lasting compost screen.**

Figure 9-2: Compost screen.

Screening small and large amounts of compost

The screening process is easy. First put on some gloves and, if you have allergies or respiratory issues, a face dust mask. (Chapter 3 discusses gloves, masks, and other gear.) Spread compost over the screen. Push it back and forth with a shovel, trowel, or your hands. Finely textured, finished compost will fall through the screen. Dump the leftovers back into the compost pile to decompose further if needed, or spread them as mulch around landscape plants (refer to the earlier section "Using Compost to Mulch Landscape Plants and Trees" for instructions).

 For small amounts of screened compost, a garden sieve held over a bucket may be sufficient. But rather than using your kitchen colander, buy one at a thrift store or garage sale so you don't have to sterilize it after use. Also, you can collect small batches of screened compost in plastic kitty litter or laundry detergent buckets with lids. Empty the containers first, of course, and then sift the compost directly into the bucket, secure the lid, and store until needed.

For large amounts, make or buy a compost screen that fits conveniently over a wheelbarrow or garden cart that's easy for you to move around where you plan to use the compost. Another option is a screen that fits over the top of one of your existing compost bins. Screen sifted compost onto a tarp spread at the base of the bin. When you're ready to use the screened compost, it's easy to lift and transport elsewhere.

Using screened compost in container plantings

Only use your own compost for containers if you have cultivated a "hot" heap to destroy weed seeds. If you plan to mix compost into potting soil for containers, I suggest screening it first because growing media for containers should be lightweight — almost fluffy — with excellent drainage. Screened compost helps create that.

A top-dressing of screened compost also lends an attractive, polished look to highly visible container gardens, such as flower pots greeting visitors by the front door and fragrant herb bowls next to patio chairs. After you've planted your containers, layer 1 inch (2.5 centimeters) of screened compost on top of the soil as mulch. This conserves soil moisture and moderates soil temperature. Throughout the growing season, replenish this layer as needed.

Finding Other Uses for Finished Compost

If you've distributed compost to every possible plant and container on your property and still have plenty to spare, you may enjoy experimenting with a batch of compost tea or growing plants directly in your compost pile.

Brewing (and using) compost tea

Compost tea — made by steeping finished compost in unheated water — has many enthusiastic advocates for its benefits as a liquid fertilizer or disease fighter for plants. Interestingly, many of the accepted truths about compost tea are gardener testimonials rather than results of scientific study. This doesn't mean that compost tea users didn't achieve desirable results (that also merit further study) or that compost tea shouldn't be part of your gardening endeavors. But I think it's good to realize upfront that many of those fantastic claims about compost tea haven't been backed up by science.

Rather than adding "brew compost tea" to your busy to-do list, you may decide it's easier to use your lovely finished compost for the other purposes I explain in this chapter. Considerable research backs up those beneficial results! If you choose to make and use compost tea, please heed the following warning.

Spraying compost tea on edible food crops is not recommended because of the potential to spread harmful bacteria or pesticide residue, depending on original compost ingredients. Don't make tea from finished compost that included manures of any kind. Manure may introduce *Escherichia coli (E. coli)* bacteria, which can spread to humans and cause extreme illness and, in some cases, death.

You can brew compost tea *aerobically* (by introducing oxygen) or *anaerobically* (without oxygen). (Flip to Chapter 4 for more details on the differences between aerobic and anaerobic composting.) Aerobic steeping churns the water to introduce oxygen, which you can do fairly simply in a home system with an aquarium pump and *air stone.* Porous air stones are used with air pumps to diffuse a cascade of bubbles through water to promote aeration. You can purchase air stones at aquarium supply outlets. Compost tea made aerobically, just like compost made aerobically in a heap or bin, should not exude bad odors.

Steeping tea anaerobically, as I describe next, involves the fewest materials and the least labor, so it's the easiest way to get your feet wet if you want to become a compost brewmeister. Be forewarned that the process and result is smelly, so you should take that into account when deciding where to set up your brewing station.

To mix up a batch of anaerobic compost tea, you need the following materials:

✔ **Finished, screened compost** (refer to the earlier section "Screening Compost for Containers" for instructions)

When brewing, never use compost that is partially decomposed; it smells worse than using finished compost and may contain harmful bacteria.

✔ **A burlap bag, an old pillowcase, pantyhose, or other porous material**

✔ **A bucket, garbage can, or other container**

Here are the steps for making compost tea anaerobically:

1. **Fill your container with water, and let it sit overnight in the open container to release chlorine.**

2. **Put compost in a porous bag, tie the bag securely, and soak it in your container of water for several days until the water turns dark brown, like strong tea.**

   Use about one shovelful of finished compost per 10 to 15 gallons (38 to 57 liters) of water.

3. **Remove the bag of compost and empty the contents (the compost) around plants, or put it back into the compost pile.**

4. **Add water to the compost tea left in the container until it's pale, like weak tea.**

   Add water to the original container if there's space, or pour the strong tea into other containers and then add plain water.

5. **Use the diluted tea to water plants, or dilute the tea further if you're watering tender seedlings or using it as a foliar spray on inedible plants.**

Growing plants directly on the pile

One of my favorite Arizona desert summertime gardening memories involves a lineup of three compost bins made of wooden shipping pallets (see Chapter 6) at the county cooperative extension compost demonstration area. Not being terribly enthused about turning tons of organic matter in ten different bins during Phoenix's triple-digit heat, my fellow lone Master Composter volunteer and I planted these side-by-side bins with gourd seeds. Rambling gourd vines, which grow 30 feet (9 meters) long without breaking a sweat quickly engulfed the bins, hiding them from view. To visitors who didn't realize what was supporting the vines, it looked like other-worldly greenery in the shape of a large rectangular block.

You don't have to be a desert dweller to try this. Simply put two or three plants such as cukes, melons, squash, pumpkins, or gourds in the center of your compost bin, water, and get out of the way!

 If your compost concoction isn't well decomposed, make a hole about the size of a bucket in the top center of the bin; fill it with soil, and plant in that.

Supply water and care as needed, depending on your local growing conditions. When the season is over and the fruits harvested, chop up the greenery and toss it back in the bin as a convenient supply of nitrogen.

Combining Homemade with Store-Bought Compost

Even the most dedicated composting gurus occasionally need more well-rotted organic matter than waits in the backyard. The good news for gardeners is that there's plenty of compost for sale that you can mix with your homemade product. The bad news is that quality of store-bought compost swings widely from excellent to "Why did I bother transporting this stuff home?"

 Because of its weight and transportation costs, most compost is made locally or regionally from organic wastes available seasonally. That's great for earth-friendly sustainability. However, because there are no standardized testing or labeling requirements for compost, you need to scrutinize it before buying.

The following sections look at bagged and bulk compost individually, but for both types you can use the low-tech "touch and sniff" method to get an idea of quality. Here's what to look for when purchasing compost in bags or bulk:

- ✔ **Texture:** It should be crumbly and fine as it runs through your fingers, with no recognizable materials. It's okay to recognize organic matter in your home batches, but not in a purchased product, which signifies it wasn't given time to decompose sufficiently. Watch out for bags labeled as compost that really contain mulch, with lots of twigs and wood chips.

- ✔ **Color:** Look for deep brown or almost black compost. Leave tan compost on the shelf.

- ✔ **Moisture:** Good-quality compost is moist, but not overly wet. Squeeze a handful. It should feel like a damp, wrung-out sponge.

- ✔ **Aroma:** Earthy, aromatic compost is easier to make than buy in plastic bags, which inhibit air circulation. But definitely avoid products with any unpleasant odors, such as ammonia, rotten eggs, or general sourness.

In terms of mixing homemade and store-bought compost, there aren't any hard and fast rules to follow. If you have the time and energy to mix the two together before using the compost, go for it. But there aren't any major benefits to be had by mixing first. Your plants, trees, and more shouldn't suffer from receiving only store-bought compost or a mixture of store-bought and homemade.

Purchasing bags of compost

Nurseries and garden centers sell compost in plastic bags. On the positive side, bags are convenient to transport and stockpile if you don't use all the compost immediately. On the other hand, bags are a tad pricey if you need large quantities and, as I explain earlier, the content varies widely.

If organic or sustainable gardening principles are important to you, look for "organic certified" or some similar statement on the bag. Beware: The word "organic" alone may simply be a descriptive term that the ingredients were once-living things. In my experience, finding certified organic compost in bags is difficult. Availability may be a function of the type of ingredients where you live and what sustainability issues are important to your local community.

You may also want to look for the words "peat-free" on the bag. Many packaged composts have peat as a main ingredient, which is harvested from peat bogs that are a fast-dwindling natural resource. There are now good, reliable, peat-free composts on sale that won't trouble your conscience.

 If you plan on purchasing a lot of bags of compost, ask store personnel to open one bag so you can ensure the quality is what you expect before you haul it home.

Buying in bulk

Buying in bulk is less expensive than bags, especially if you load and haul it yourself. Some sellers transport it to your home for a fee. Ask the suppliers if they offer "dumpy bags" (an option in the United Kingdom, whereby compost is delivered in 1-cubic-meter bags) that are easier to handle than a large mound piled unceremoniously on your driveway. In the United States, bulk producers and suppliers usually price compost in dollars per cubic yard, but make sure you're comparing apples to apples. (To help you visualize, 1 cubic yard (1 cubic meter) of compost covers 324 square feet at 1 inch (2.5 centimeters) thick; 2 cubic yards (2 cubic meters) of compost fills most standard pick-up truck beds.)

Bulk compost operators may offer a variety of grades from which to choose, such as screened compost, compost mixed with topsoil, or mulching compost. (Don't confuse the latter with traditional mulch, which is chipped bark that's not suitable for digging into the soil.) Screened compost is finer, more uniform in texture, and more expensive than other grades. If possible, go to the site and examine the compost to ensure you're getting what you want.

Consider asking these questions when purchasing from a compost producer:

- ✔ **What is it made of?** Who supplied the original materials? Is it organic certified? Avoid materials that may have been sprayed with chemical pesticides, such as agricultural crops, or may contain some animal manure. (Chapter 7 covers issues related to manure use in compost.)

- ✔ **How do you process it?** Bulk composters can explain their composting method. You want to hear something such as "turned every two weeks for 16 weeks and aerobically processed at 140 degrees Fahrenheit (60 degrees Celsius) to kill potential weed seeds and pathogens." If their process is unclear, and they aren't too sure about the original ingredients, you may want to pass up this compost to reduce the chance of transporting weed seeds or pathogens home!

✔ **Do you test the end results?** Bulk operators may be able to provide information such as moisture content, organic matter content, pH, salt content, and nutrient levels, including NPK (nitrogen, phosphorus, potassium). Look for moisture content in the 35 to 55 percent range, pH levels between 5.5 and 7.5, and salt below 5 mho/centimeter. (Mho is a unit to measure salt conductivity. Excessive soil salts are harmful to most plants, especially young seedlings.) NPK ratios are typically quite low for compost, so don't be concerned about those numbers.

Part IV
Expanding Your Compost Horizons

The 5th Wave   By Rich Tennant

"I built the worm bin myself. They seem to like the chandelier overhead, but we're replacing the sconces over the fireplace with recessed mood spots."

In this part . . .

*B*uilding and maintaining a compost pile isn't your only option for recycling your household's organic waste and adding organic matter to your garden's soil. This part looks at alternatives, starting with vermicomposting, a method in which hard-working red wiggler worms transform your kitchen waste into plant nutrients and soil amendment.

You also can select and grow a cover crop or green manure, and then incorporate it directly into the soil to boost levels of organic matter and nutrients. I explain this age-old practice, which is experiencing an increase in popularity along with increased interest in organic gardening methods. I also introduce you to sheet composting — spreading layers of organic matter on top of your soil to decompose right where compost is needed — and offer an easy-to-follow method for improving soil and planting in one swoop.

Chapter 10

Working with Worms

. . . .

. . . .

*1*magine eating enough food every day to equal half your weight. That's what red wiggler worms do, making them the perfect choice for vermicomposting.

Vermicomposting is a composting method that employs certain worm species to consume and convert organic matter into a useful soil amendment and organic fertilizer. These composting worms thrive in varied situations, including a simple indoor container that recycles your household food scraps or in sophisticated operations designed to handle school cafeteria waste or process large quantities of animal manure from farms.

In this chapter, I stick with the basics of an indoor household worm bin to recycle kitchen waste. It's a fine composting method if you don't have outdoor garden space and want to recycle your food scraps rather than send them to a landfill or down the garbage disposal. Even if you have a garden, using a worm composter will enable you to recycle cooked food scraps that can't go on a normal compost heap.

You'll find everything you need to know to start an indoor vermicomposting system, including descriptions of the worm species and step-by-step instructions for constructing a bin to house them. I explain how to feed and maintain healthy worms and offer troubleshooting tips. The chapter concludes with suggestions for harvesting and using their rich compost.

Vermicomposting in a Nutshell

A worm's digestive tract extends the entire length of its body. Worm food passes through it to be excreted as *castings* — a refined term for worm poop. Pure castings resemble grains of black soil or coffee grounds. In your worm bin, castings blend with partially decomposed food scraps and worm bedding to form *vermicompost*. It has many benefits similar to those of "regular" compost. When added to soil, vermicompost improves aeration, water retention, porosity, and microbial activity. Vermicompost also suppresses diseases in plants and enhances plant growth.

To give credit where credit is due, the worms are not producing this great product on their own. The same types of decomposer microorganisms that work in an outdoor compost pile are also at work in a vermicomposting system. Worms consume microorganisms along with bits of plant material, so they, too, end up in your rich vermicompost.

Vermicomposting is a *mesophilic* process, meaning it takes place at medium temperatures. (Chapter 3 covers more details on preferred temperature ranges of composting organisms.) Worms and their helper microorganisms generate temperatures ranging from 50 to 90 degrees Fahrenheit (10 to 32 degrees Celsius). Vermicomposting isn't viable in large, deep compost piles (1 cubic yard [1 cubic meter] or greater) that self-insulate and heat up to hot or *thermophilic* temperatures. Lots of horizontal surface area, about 8 to 12 inches (20 to 30 centimeters) deep, works best for vermicomposting.

Vermicomposting has far more pros than cons. I admit that it may not be right for you if you're not fond of worms. Also, if not well managed, a vermicompost bin may attract pesky vinegar flies. But the pros far outnumber these cons and include the following:

✔ It requires very little space.

✔ Apartment and condo dwellers can compost their food scraps.

✔ It reduces the amount of organic waste sent to landfills.

✔ It reduces trash collection fees based on volume.

✔ It creates a premium-quality soil amendment.

✔ It's a great way to teach kids about recycling and life cycles.

✔ It requires very little physical labor or strength.

✔ It reduces water and electricity usage by eliminating the need to run an in-sink garbage disposal.

✔ It produces less odor and attracts fewer pests than scraps left in garbage cans.

Meet the Squirmy Stars of the Show

Thousands of worm species exist, but only a remarkable few species work effectively as vermicomposters. Don't buy random worms from bait shops or even dig them up from your garden. They won't be the right sort of heavy-duty consumers required to process kitchen waste fast and furiously.

Composting worm species

The most commonly sold worm for vermicomposting in the United States and Canada is the *red wiggler (Eisenia fetida)*. Other common names it answers to include *brandling worm, manure worm,* or *red-worm*. Another composting worm less commonly available is *Eisenia andreii,* sometimes called the *tiger worm*. In the United Kingdom, composting worms are sometimes sold as a "mix" with two or three species. Throughout this chapter, I refer to red wigglers because they're the most common choice for vermicomposting.

In nature, red wigglers thrive in such delightfully rich and moist living environments as farm animal manure patties or decomposing plant debris beneath fallen logs. They don't tunnel into deep or permanent burrows in the ground, preferring to hang out close to the surface where the really good rotten stuff is readily available. Because of their proficiency at consuming lots of organic matter and their preference for shallow living quarters, they're well suited to life in shallow, household vermicomposting systems. (See "Hooking Up the Housing and Bedding" later in this chapter for details.)

Obtaining composting worms

Buy from worm suppliers who label their products by genus and species (such as *Eisenia fetida*), rather than common names, which vary from place to place. You don't want to go home with worms that aren't suited to the task or with potentially invasive species.

Concern exists that non-native worm species, such as *Lumbricus rubellus,* a European red worm sometimes used for composting, may be invading North American forests and consuming leaf litter so rapidly that they're changing the nutrient cycles. Numerous plant and animal species rely on a typical thick mat of organic matter that decays slowly over many years. When the organic matter is consumed quickly and disappears, so does the lifeblood of the ecosystem. Even if you carefully pick out live worms before spreading vermicompost in your garden, it's likely to have a few cocoons with babies ready to hatch and go on walkabout. Obtain your composting worms labeled by genus and species and check with local experts for concerns about invasive species in your area.

Ask friends and co-workers for someone who already has a vermicompost bin. Happy red wigglers in their favored environment reproduce regularly. Most successful vermicomposters are delighted to "thin their herd" because overpopulation creates problems, as it does for any other species.

Worms are typically sold by the pound in the United States and Canada. In the United Kingdom, they're sold by the kilo, or fractions thereof. One pound averages about 1,000 worms, although the actual count varies depending on the relative size and age of individuals. A pound of worms is more than plenty for most households to get started.

Hooking Up the Housing and Bedding

Wild composting worms live in Mother Nature's top layers of soil and leaf litter. They don't thrive deep in the ground, as some other worm species do. In your home vermicomposting system, all you have to do is duplicate their preferred shallow living conditions with a bin that offers lots of surface area (rather than great depth) and keep it loaded with moist bedding.

How much room do your worms need?

How big of a bin you need (and how many worms to put in it) depends on how much kitchen waste you have to process. Review the list of acceptable worm food later in the chapter and estimate the weight of worm food your household generates. Weighing your kitchen scraps for a week to get a rough idea is helpful.

These points help you estimate your bin size:

- ✔ Composting worms work well in depths of 8 to 12 inches (20 to 30 centimeters).

- ✔ Provide 1 square foot (0.3 square meter) of surface area for each pound of garbage to be composted. For two people, a bin that is 2 feet long by 2 feet wide by 8 inches deep (60 x 60 x 20 centimeters) is generally adequate.

- ✔ Plan on worms consuming about half their weight per day: 1 pound (0.5 kilogram) of worms eats ½ pound (0.2 kilogram) of scraps; 2 pounds (1 kilogram) of worms eat 1 pound (0.5 kilogram) of scraps, and so on. They may eat more than this, but err on the side of caution so as to not overwhelm your bin residents and create problems.

With a brand new vermicomposting endeavor, it may take your worms a few days or even weeks to get up to speed, so be careful not to overfeed them. It's easy to add more scraps if they're plowing through your initial offerings, but it's not much fun to remove excess scraps or deal with the problems that an overload can cause, such as odors or vinegar flies.

Building your own worm abode

In my experience, as long as they have appropriate aeration, moisture, and food, worms aren't concerned about where they eat and poop. Bin aesthetics is a human requirement!

If you're interested in constructing a home for your worms instead of buying one, I suggest starting out with a simple and inexpensive plastic storage bin or bins. They're available in numerous sizes and shapes that will suit your worms just fine — you can even reuse ones that you already have. Plastic storage bins allow you to decide whether vermicomposting suits your household with a minimal investment of time and money.

The double-decker design shown in Figure 10-1 includes a built-in method for harvesting vermicompost. If you prefer to get your feet wet with just one bin, follow the basic drilling instructions for the double-decker bin, substituting one bin. (You still need two lids: one for a lid and one for a drip tray.)

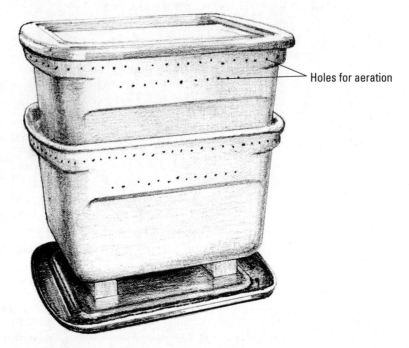

Holes for aeration

Figure 10-1: Double-decker vermicomposting bins.

The materials for the double-decker worm bin include

- 2 plastic storage containers with lids. Bins should be dark and opaque, because worms can't tolerate light.
- A drill with ¼-inch (6.35 millimeter) and ¹⁄₁₆-inch (1.58 millimeter) bits.
- 2 bricks to set bin above floor level.

Construct your bin by following these steps:

1. **Using the ¼-inch (6.35 millimeter) drill bit, make 20 holes evenly spaced in the bottom of each bin.**

   These holes allow drainage so conditions won't become too wet, and they promote aeration, which is essential to an aerobic composting environment. When it's time to harvest castings, your worms will travel through the holes from one bin into the other (see Step 5.)

2. **Using the ¹⁄₁₆-inch (1.58 millimeter) bit, drill smaller aeration holes every 1 to 2 inches (2.5 to 5 centimeters) on each side of each bin near the top edge.**

3. **Using the ¹⁄₁₆-inch (1.58 millimeter) bit, drill about 30 small holes in the top of one of the lids to allow for aeration.**

    Leave the second lid without holes to act as a tray to catch drips.

4. **Set the drip tray on the floor. Position the two bricks on the tray to provide good balance when one full bin is set on top.**

    Raising the worm bin several inches off the floor with bricks promotes air flow beneath it.

5. **Add the second bin when you're ready to harvest finished vermicompost (see the section "Slow harvest method" later in the chapter for instructions).**

Opting for a manufactured worm bin

Increased interest in vermicomposting is mirrored by an increase in the variety of manufactured worm bins available in recent years. You can find them at garden stores or order them through garden catalogs and online retailers, such as the National Gardening Association, www.garden.org, or Peaceful Valley Farm & Garden Supply, www.groworganic.com.

Obviously, a manufactured bin will cost you a bit more than recycling a free plastic storage container (see the preceding section for instructions). Bins can range in price from $50 to $175.

In their natural environment, composting worms live at or near the soil surface. They don't dive deep into the ground, so lots of shallow surface area is more important than a deep container. That's why most manufactured worm bins are made with some style of multiple, shallow stacking shelves. They offer increased surface area within the unit's overall relatively small footprint.

Follow the earlier suggestions under "Building your own worm abode" for estimating the amount of your kitchen scraps and the number of worms you'll need to consume it. Compare that to the manufacturer's specifications for how many worms a given product houses or how much kitchen waste it will hold to find the most suitable size.

Stacked designs allow worms to do what comes naturally: move upwards to seek food. Start worms with bedding and food in the bottom tray. After they finish decomposing that section, offer food and bedding in the next tray, and up they'll go, leaving vermicompost behind to cure until you harvest it.

Some worm bins have spigots to drain liquid. However, liquid that leaks from the bottom of a worm bin is not vermicompost tea. It's *leachate*, or excess liquid that flows through organic matter. Because it's an extract of undigested materials, it may contain pathogens harmful to plants. True vermicompost tea is made by steeping finished (digested) vermicompost in water.

Making the bed

Provide moist bedding at all times for your worms to romp around in while they process your organic matter. They have no lungs or gills and breathe through their skin, which they coat with mucous. Dissolved oxygen passes through their skin into the bloodstream. Worms must live in moist, humid surroundings because if their skin dries out, they die.

Over time, worms consume their bedding along with your food scraps, but that's okay. By then, you'll be ready to harvest castings and provide fresh bedding.

Making bedding for your worms requires only two materials: two handfuls of native soil and newspaper or computer paper. You may also use leaves and shredded cardboard for bedding, either in place of paper or in addition to it. I prefer newspaper because there's always plenty of it around to be recycled, and it's easy to work with.

Follow these steps to make your worms the sort of bedding they'll never want to leave:

1. **Wash bins thoroughly before adding bedding and worms.**

2. **Tear paper into 1-inch (2.5-centimeter) strips.**

   Fill one side of your sink with water. Soak the paper in it. Lift it out and let excess water drain in the other side of the sink. Don't squeeze the paper because then it will dry into hard chunks.

3. **Lightly place the paper in the bin.**

   Composting worms work in 8 to 12 inches (20 to 30 centimeters) of bedding depth. Fill the bin at least 12 inches (30 centimeters) deep because the bedding will settle a bit. Fluff up the bedding so that it's loose, with air pockets, rather than compacted.

4. **Sprinkle two handfuls of your native soil into the bedding.**

   This provides grit for the worms' digestive process and adds microorganisms to aid with decomposition.

5. Bury one handful of food scraps in the bedding.

Don't overwhelm red wigglers with too much food in the first week while they're getting acclimated. When these scraps are gone, add more, gradually working up to greater quantities. (The next section explains what worms like to eat.)

Introducing worms to their new home

Place your red wigglers on top of the moist bedding and they'll begin disappearing into it. If they seem slow to go, shine a bright light above the bin. They should dive for the dark depths.

Chow Time! Feeding Your Worms

Vermicomposting worms in your indoor bin eat the same organic goodies that you add to an outdoor compost pile, including spent garden plants, landscape trimmings, scrap paper, and kitchen scraps. However, I assume that you'll feed them kitchen scraps.

Mentally divide your bin into "zones," and bury food scraps in different sections of the bin with each feeding.

Plan on feeding your worms about half their weight in food scraps per day. When starting a new bin, offer just a handful of food until they get acclimated and start digging into your provisions. As a general guideline, feed your worms when the majority of the previous food has disappeared.

What's on the menu

The more variety in ingredients, the better the vermicompost. Try not to overload your worm bin with fruit and vegetable skins, which may attract vinegar flies. Also, avoid lots of salty food waste, which will dry out the poor little worms. Everything in moderation!

Worms are known to have food preferences (really), so experiment to see what your red wigglers prefer. Here's a hint: sweet mushy stuff like melon, pumpkin, and squash is popular at my house. Other good additions include

- ✔ Raw or cooked vegetables
- ✔ Coffee grounds and filters
- ✔ Tea and paper tea bags

✔ Stale bread and grain products

✔ Ground-up eggshells

✔ Fruit rinds and cores

Add citrus in very small amounts so the bin doesn't become too acidic. (See the section "pH levels" later in the chapter for more details.)

Put apple cores in your worm bin. They will soon have worms sticking out of them, just like the drawings in children's books. Kids think this is a hoot!

Just as there are items that shouldn't be added to a regular compost pile, the following items aren't appropriate worm food:

✔ **Meat, fish, or dairy:** These foodstuffs may turn rancid and smelly as they decompose, as well as attract undesirables such as houseflies or vinegar flies (also called fruit flies).

✔ **Greases and oils:** Worms breathe through their skin. Oils and grease coat their skin and prevent them from breathing.

✔ **Pet or human waste:** It may contain pathogens that are transmitted to humans.

To chop or not to chop (again)

Chopping scraps into 2- to 4-inch (5- to 10-centimeter) bits speeds the decomposition process in your vermicomposting bin, just as it does in your outdoor compost pile. However, it isn't always essential if you're in a hurry and your bin has been functioning well. Worms can execute with impressive alacrity on large chunks of food waste. I once plunked a flavorless half cantaloupe into my bin upside down without chopping — seedy pulp, flesh, rind, and all. Within two days, my Wormingtons stripped it down to a paper-thin sheet of rind that displayed a delicate ribbed pattern when I held it up to the light. Efficient little critters, those red wigglers.

Maintaining Your Worms' Comfort Zone

In addition to bedding and food, worms need appropriate temperature, moisture, oxygen, and pH levels to thrive. And they don't like the lights left on!

Light

Worms don't have eyes, but they're still extremely sensitive to light and move away from bright light if they can. If exposed to bright light for an hour, some worms become paralyzed. Unable to move away, they dry out and die. Put your bin in a dark location, keep a lid on it, or throw a towel or other covering over it to block light.

Temperature

The optimal temperature range for red wigglers is from 55 to 77 degrees Fahrenheit (13 to 25 degrees Celsius). You can stretch those limits from 50 to 84 degrees Fahrenheit (10 to 29 degrees Celsius), but they may not process as much organic matter or reproduce as vigorously.

Moisture

Maintaining moist bedding is crucial. Worm bedding should be 60 to 85 percent moisture. Depending on what types of food scraps you supply, the bedding may remain moist. But I've always had to add moisture by misting with a water spray bottle or sprinkling drops of water across the bed periodically.

On the other hand, don't let the bin become a swamp. Wet conditions turn the bin into a smelly anaerobic composting system. (If you read Chapter 4, you know that anaerobic composting is stinky!)

Worms must remain in a moist, humid environment at all times, or they will die.

Breathing room

Red wigglers need oxygen to maintain their household as an aerobic (with air), sweet-smelling system. Be careful not to allow bedding to become too wet or to add too much food at once, which may deplete oxygen levels. Once a week or so, aerate the bedding by gently fluffing it up. If you're squeamish about worms, wear rubber gloves or use a big plastic spoon or spatula to gently lift and turn.

pH levels

pH is a measure of acidity and alkalinity on a scale from 1 to 14. Acidic is 1 to 6; alkaline is 8 to 14; 7 is neutral. In nature, worms survive in a range of pH levels, but in the small space of your bin, it's best to keep pH in the range of 6.8 to 7.2.

Does that mean you have to measure pH levels? Not unless you want to. I never measure the pH level in a worm bin. I mention it in case you experience problems and more obvious troubleshooting methods don't correct them. The following food adjustments can help you maintain pH levels that don't jump out of whack:

- ✔ Limit the amount of citrus scraps to prevent the bin from getting too acidic.

- ✔ Add crushed eggshells to lower acidity.

- ✔ Limit the amount of nitrogen-rich materials that rapidly decompose, such as an abundance of coffee grounds. Nitrogen materials release ammonia and increase pH levels.

If you're interested in testing the pH of your worm bin, garden stores and online retailers sell various styles of simple pH testing kits, such as a paper strips, capsules, or meters. Although not always extremely precise, they'll provide you with a troubleshooting guide.

Tackling Problems with Your Worm Bin

If you follow the guidelines in this chapter, your vermicomposting efforts should be successful. But just in case you encounter problems, Table 10-1 and the following sections address a few issues that sometimes crop up.

Table 10-1 Troubleshooting Problems in Worm Bins	
Worm Bin Problem	**Probable Cause**
Vinegar flies	Food scraps exposed; overfeeding, especially citrus fruit
Bad odors	Food scraps exposed; bedding too wet; insufficient aeration; overfeeding

Worm Bin Problem	Probable Cause
Worms crawling away or dying	Bedding too wet or dry; insufficient food or aeration; temperatures too hot or cold; conditions too acidic or salty
Water collecting in bin	Poor drainage or ventilation; food scraps too watery
Mold forming	Conditions too acidic
Bedding drying out	Too much ventilation

Odor

Most likely the bedding is too wet and compacted and your aerobic (with air) vermicomposting operation has turned anaerobic (without air). Chapter 4 describes the anaerobic decomposers as the microorganisms who give off stinky gas as a byproduct of their exertions. If conditions aren't too bad, you may be able to blend in dry bedding to soak up excess moisture. If the bedding is a black, icky mess, salvage the worms, clean the bin, and start anew with fresh bedding.

Mites

As Chapter 3 describes, mites are part of the vast network of decomposer organisms, and small populations of mites are common in vermicomposting systems. However, if mite populations leap out of control, they can become hazardous to your worms' health. The best way to avoid a mite problem is to take good care of the worm bin, providing appropriate aeration, moisture, and food. Overly wet beds, an overabundance of food, and foods with high moisture content all favor mites.

Dying worms

Worm bodies are composed mostly of water. When worms die naturally, you're unlikely to notice any worm carcasses because they decompose so quickly. However, if you see lots of dead worms all at once, it's time to investigate the cause. It's probably best to harvest healthy worms, wash out the bin, and start with fresh bedding.

What Worms Contribute to Your Compost: The Casting Call

Castings are the materials that have traveled through the worms' digestive systems and come out the other end as excrement. Castings resemble dark bits of soil or coffee grounds. Incorporated with the castings will be bits of bedding and food scraps that are more or less decomposed, worms, and maybe worm cocoons holding babies. The entire mix is referred to as *vermicompost.*

Just as your outdoor compost pile shrinks in size over time, so does the worms' bedding. It becomes darker in color, unrecognizable as its original substance, and more "compost-like." Castings also amass in the bin, which creates a toxic environment for the red wigglers. Think about it. They're living in poop. That can't go on indefinitely, so it's important for you to harvest the vermicompost and prepare fresh bedding.

As a guideline, change the bedding and harvest castings every four to six months. Your bin may last for six months without harvesting, but when you're first gaining experience, monitor your bin for signs that life is stressful, such as the worm population diminishing, food disappearing less quickly, or an absence of cocoons with babies on the way. If those conditions exist, it's time to harvest your vermicompost (see the next section) and provide fresh bedding.

Harvesting vermicompost

In this section I give you two methods for harvesting vermicompost. One method is based on the worms' desire to eat; the other takes advantage of their dislike of bright light.

When harvesting vermicompost, you may notice shiny, yellowish to light brown structures shaped like ⅛-inch-long grape seeds, with one pointy end and the other round. These are worm cocoons, holding 2 to 20 baby worms each. Transfer cocoons to the fresh bin with the worms.

Slow harvest method

This method of harvesting vermicompost is more passive on your part than the quick harvest method I cover in the next section. Here, you basically wait for the worms to move toward the food (kind of like party guests moving toward a buffet table!). If you buy or make a tiered bin like the one in Figure 10-1, the worms will move from bottom levels upwards to consume fresh supplies of food, and you'll be able to simply empty out the finished compost in the lowest tier.

Follow these steps for the slow harvest method using your double-decker bins as shown in Figure 10-1:

1. **When you're ready to harvest castings from the first bin, place fresh moist bedding material in the second bin.**

2. **Remove the lid from the first bin, and set the fresh bin directly on the vermicompost surface of the first bin. Put the lid on the fresh bin.**

3. **Bury all new food scraps in the fresh bin. Gradually, most worms will relocate to the fresh bin in search of food because it's their nature to head to the surface to feed. This may take two to four weeks (or maybe longer). Poke around in the bins periodically to monitor their activity.**

4. **After most worms have made the move, harvest vermi-compost from the first bin.**

5. **Remove any leftover worms and put them in the second bin.**

If you choose to vermicompost with a single bin, the same principle of harvesting applies: Worms head for the chow line, so put food scraps on one side of the bin. After they've traveled over to that side, harvest the vacated vermicompost, and repeat the process on the other side.

Quick harvest method

With the quick harvest method, you, umm, encourage your worms to get a move on by dumping them out of their bin and into the light. Their natural aversion to light works in your favor. Follow these steps to use the quick method of harvesting vermicompost:

1. **Spread a plastic tarp or old shower curtain where it can stay conveniently for several hours in bright light — either sunlight or artificial light.**

2. **Dump the entire contents of your bin onto the tarp in a pyramid-shaped pile (wide at the base, peaked at the top).**

   Worms at the top and outer edges begin diving into the compost depths to get away from the light.

3. **While waiting for the worms to get a move on, refill their bin with fresh, moist bedding (see the earlier section "Making the bed" for bedding instructions). Bury about half the food scraps you normally supply.**

   The upheaval of a move is stressful, so allow them time to adjust rather than overfeeding.

4. **After 15 to 30 minutes, gently scrape off the top layers of vermicompost, which should be mostly worm-free.**

   Pick out any stragglers, and move them to the fresh bin. Reshape the pyramid. Wait for more worms to dive into the depths.

5. **Repeat this process as many times as needed, until you reach the base of the pyramid.**

   At this point, it will be mostly a mass of red wigglers, which you can pick up and transfer to the fresh bin.

Remember worm bodies must stay moist so they can breathe, or they will die. Be sure you don't forget about them in harsh light. Set your watch or kitchen timer to ring every 15 minutes. If harvesting outdoors, monitor the pile to fend off any plundering birds.

Observing worms at work

My first worm bin was a homemade wooden box with one Plexiglas side so the Wormingtons could be observed when their little bodies were pressed up against the glass.

The Plexiglas "viewing station," although interesting, was only marginally effective for showcasing the worms during composting workshops because as soon as I removed the cloth that kept the bin in the dark, the worms disappeared lickety-split into the depths of their bedding. You'd think they were being hunted by hungry robins rather living a life of luxury where all they had to do was occasionally let interested people stare at them.

Viewing worms often causes great excitement among kids and starts them down a path of natural discovery. If you decide to create a viewing room for your budding vermicomposters, remember that worms can't stand light and will die if overexposed. Be sure to keep the bin in a dark place or cover it with something that blocks all light.

Using vermicompost

Rich vermicompost is much desired by savvy gardeners and plant growers. Although actual nutrient content of vermicompost varies depending on the types of food and bedding that the worms eat, tests show that vermicompost contains 5 to 11 times more calcium, magnesium, nitrogen, phosphorus, and potassium than plain soil. All those nutrients contribute to healthy plant growth.

Castings provide beneficial microbial activity that combats plant disease, and they contain growth hormones that promote seed germination. Castings are lightweight, almost spongy. When added to soil as an amendment, castings improve aeration and water-holding capacity.

Vermicompost can be applied in the same ways you use finished compost from a typical outdoor composting system, such as mulching around plants, top-dressing lawns, or mixing it into flower and vegetable beds. If initial quantities are limited, use your vermicompost to top-dress your favorite houseplants or put it to use where you can maximize its benefits, such as adding it to soil mix for container plants. Remove any worms or cocoons, because the living conditions in pots aren't suited for them.

Chapter 11

Adding Cover Crops and Green Manures

Despite their name, *cover crops* aren't grown to harvest for human or animal consumption like other crops. Instead, they're planted to protect the soil and improve its quality. If you're just getting underway with composting efforts or you don't have sufficient organic matter to generate compost to meet all your gardening needs, consider planting a cover crop as a way to improve the soil or to produce composting ingredients.

In this chapter, I define the slight difference between a cover crop and its green manure cousin, and then I cover the numerous benefits that they offer to enhance your soil-building endeavors. Ultimately, they lead you to a healthier, more productive garden, providing the same perks you'd achieve by adding compost. I also give recommendations on what and when to plant by geographic region, and I include directions for incorporating the crops into your soil, basically allowing them to compost in place.

Recognizing the Value of Cover Crops and Green Manures

Cover crop and *green manure* are terms that often are used interchangeably. Indeed, the same plant choices are grown for either purpose, and they provide similar, long lists of improvements to your soil. To simplify matters, I use the term "cover crop" throughout this chapter, but here's an explanation of their slightly different usages:

- ✔ **Cover crops** are typically sown to prevent soil erosion and inhibit weed growth when a garden area is left unplanted during its dormant season. "Covering" the soil with vegetation reduces erosion from wind, rainfall, and snowmelt. Crop roots also hang onto soil particles, holding valuable topsoil in place.

- ✔ **Green manures** are typically sown to increase nitrogen availability and add organic matter to the soil during the growing season.

Although those slight differences in definition exist, in practice, the same plant species may be grown as a cover crop or a green manure. In the remainder of this section, I describe the numerous benefits cover crops bring to your composting and soil-building activities.

Preventing erosion

It may happen more gradually than you take note of it, but the combination of wind and runoff from rain and snowmelt gradually erodes your garden's topsoil — which harbors essential nutrients and organic matter. A cover crop's aboveground foliage buffers soil against the relentless ravages of wind and water, while underground roots do their part to reduce erosion by holding soil particles in place. Because climate change is bringing more severe weather conditions, you can help prevent soil erosion by planting a cover crop when your garden lies fallow during its dormant season.

Adding organic matter

Organic matter improves soil structure and fertility. Chapter 3 describes the ongoing work of billions of organisms decomposing organic matter in your compost pile. Those same creatures are working in your soil, reducing organic debris into useable bits of nutrients for plants and other creatures to absorb.

It's up to you to replenish organic matter and nutrients in your garden's soil to provide an ongoing fuel source for all these creatures. One method for doing that is to incorporate compost regularly as recommended in Chapter 10. Another option is to plant a cover crop directly in your garden in advance of your planting season. Cover crops perform a role similar to that of compost, offering decaying organic matter for a host of bacteria, fungi, and other soil organisms to build a thriving soil food web.

Reducing soil compaction

Cover crops inhibit rain from splashing on bare ground, which disturbs the soil's natural texture and causes compaction. Over time, compacted soil surfaces *seal,* impeding water penetration and facilitating runoff. In addition to promoting soil erosion, water runoff carries away nutrients and may leach undesirable or toxic substances into groundwater sources.

Improving tilth

The deep, fibrous root systems of many cover crops (especially grains and grasses) penetrate widely through the soil, creating elaborate avenues for effective air and water infiltration. This in turn improves *tilth,* which refers to soil's physical ability to support plant growth. Soil with good tilth is loose, crumbly, and easy for you to dig in and work with. Deep-rooted crops are particularly useful for improving clay or silty soils.

Creating and adding nitrogen

Nitrogen is one of three essential elements that plants require to thrive. (The other two are phosphorus and potassium.) Nitrogen is in limited supply in many soils, and even if you're lucky to garden where soils are nutrient-rich, nitrogen will be depleted with repeated growing cycles if you don't replenish it with compost or fertilizer. Planting a legume cover crop, which is capable of producing its own nitrogen, also enhances nitrogen availability in your garden. (Read more about this later in the chapter in the section "Legumes" as well as in the sidebar "Fixating on nitrogen.")

Feeding beneficial insects

Cover crops offer habitat and food (in the form of pollen and nectar) for beneficial pollinators, such as bees. Without bees, mealtime would be downright boring because these exceptional creatures are responsible for pollinating one-third of the food crops that you and I consume. Cover crops also support myriad beneficial predators, including lady beetles, parasitic wasps, predatory mites, and spiders. They serve as important biological control agents to keep pest populations in check without forcing you to resort to chemical pesticides.

Inhibiting weed growth

Cover crops are sometimes referred to as "living mulch" because of their ability to out-compete weeds. Just as a layer of compost mulch spread on top of the soil deters weeds (read more about that in Chapter 9), a dense cover crop suppresses weeds by shading the soil. When sunlight is blocked, weed seeds can't germinate. Also, a thick cover crop out-competes existing weeds for sun, water, and air. If you're struggling to get weed crops under control (perhaps a previous owner of your home let things get out of hand), plant a living mulch cover crop between rows in your garden or orchard.

Surveying Your Cover Crop Choices

Cover crops fall into three categories: legumes, grasses, and a catch-all "other" category. These plants may be *annuals,* which germinate, grow, set seed, and die in one season, or they may be *perennials,* which live for many years, although they typically go dormant in your region's off-season. Regardless of grouping, cover crops exhibit some combination of the following characteristics, which make them very capable at their job. They

✔ Grow quickly to provide significant organic matter to add to the soil or compost heap

✔ Develop fibrous root systems that spread through soil

✔ Are relatively easy to cut or mow and incorporate into soil or add to the compost heap

✔ Add nitrogen

 Legume cover crops add more nitrogen to your soil, whereas grass cover crops do a better job of increasing total organic matter. Sowing a cover crop that contains both a legume and a grass provides you with the best of both.

 Many cover crops are workhorses that accept a broad range of growing conditions. Temperature is usually the limiting factor, because some won't survive cold or tolerate extreme heat. For the fast track to figuring out which cover crop to plant, contact a full-service garden nursery or your nearest farm supply store for a quick and easy answer to your cover crop conundrum. (Even most urban areas have a farm supply store or two.) Staff can advise you on what works best in your region, and they can probably find it on their shelves, too.

Legumes

Legumes are plants that produce a bean or pea pod. Common legumes in gardens or landscapes that you may already grow include French, runner, or snap beans, peas, fragrant sweet pea flowers, acacia shrubs, and mesquite trees, to name just a handful. Cover crop legumes include alfalfa, beans, clovers, peas, and trefoil.

Legume plants have a symbiotic relationship with *Rhizobia* bacteria, in which they combine efforts to convert nitrogen in the air into a form of nitrogen that plant roots can absorb in the soil. This conversion process is called *nitrogen fixation* (see the sidebar "Fixating on nitrogen" for more).

Grasses

Unlike legumes, grasses (a category that includes cereal grains, such as oats) are not capable of nitrogen fixation, although they do add plenty of organic matter to your soil when cut and turned under. Their vigorous and matting root systems also inhibit soil erosion. Cover crops in this category include annual (Italian) or perennial ryegrass, Sudangrass, oats, cereal, grazing or winter rye (which isn't the same as ryegrass), and winter wheat.

Fixating on nitrogen

All plants require nitrogen to grow. However, your soil's nitrogen levels may be in short supply because of regional characteristics or may have become depleted over time with repeated growing cycles and insufficient replenishment with compost and fertilizer. Planting a cover crop of legumes is a great way to improve your soil's nitrogen levels.

Although the atmosphere contains abundant nitrogen (almost 80 percent), it's not in a form that plants can absorb. Legumes have mastered the process of converting this "free" atmospheric nitrogen into a form that becomes available in the soil for other plants to use. Legumes can't perform this feat alone, though. In a mutually beneficial relationship, soil-dwelling *Rhizobia* bacteria assist legumes with the process of nitrogen fixation.

Within legume root nodules, bacteria produce a chemical that converts nitrogen from the air into nitrogen that the legume can absorb and use to make proteins. In exchange, the legume offers the bacteria sugars and carbohydrates for energy and continued growth. When leguminous cover crops decompose, nitrogen in their root nodules is released for other plants to use.

Other cover crops

Neither legume nor grass, buckwheat is an excellent cover crop if you need a fast-grower to out-compete weeds. It matures in 30 to 45 days in warm weather. Buckwheat tolerates low-fertility soil and thrives in warm temperatures. Other cover crops that fall into this catchall category are cabbage-family crops such as kale and mustard, fenugreek, and phacelia.

Planting and Turning Over Cover Crops

General characteristics of geographic gardening regions dictate when you should plant cover crops. This section offers guidelines for different sowing seasons, and I also give you instructions for ultimately incorporating your cover crop into the soil for decomposition (yet another great form of composting!).

Sowing seasons

When to plant cover crops depends in part on your region's gardening seasons as well as on what you want to achieve with a cover crop. Are you protecting the soil from erosion during your area's spring rainy season? If so, plant in fall so that crops are up and running by spring. Do you want to add a quick blast of nutrients to the soil before starting a new summer garden? If so, sow crops as soon as possible after your last frost date. The following information provides you with planting schedules based on general temperature and gardening seasons. Check with your favorite garden center, farm supply store, or county cooperative extension office to fine-tune your planting time.

> ✔ **Cold and/or snowy winters with one short summer growing season:** Planting period: August to late September. (Alternative planting period: After your area's last frost in spring.)
>
> Sow cover crops in time for at least four weeks of growth before cold weather halts development. Crops germinate with the last of the warm soil temperatures and produce foliage to protect soil from erosion over winter. When temperatures warm in spring, growth of perennial crops will resume. If you're waiting for optimal harvest time for vegetable crops still producing in your garden, you may sow cover crops between rows or "inter-crop" around the edges of vegetable plants.

➤ **Somewhat moderate temperatures and/or rainy winters with one longer growing season; most gardens dormant in winter:** Planting period: August through early December (Alternative planting period: After your area's last frost in spring.)

The earlier the sowing, the better established the cover crop will be because most seeds don't germinate well in cold and/ or wet soils.

➤ **Warm or hot summers with two gardening seasons or year-round gardening:** Planting period: May through June. (Alternative planting period: Before either gardening season.)

The earlier you sow seeds the better, allowing your cover crop to establish before intense heat arrives. Late sowings require more moisture to germinate and get plants off to a good start.

Mixing your mature cover crop into the soil

As a general guideline, cut down and incorporate cover crops into the soil at least one to three weeks before planting your next garden in order to allow some decomposition to occur.

Benefits achieved from your cover crop depend on how long the crop is allowed to grow before you cut and turn it under. As a general guideline, allow plants to grow for as long as possible to maximize organic mass *without* developing woody stems or seed heads. Mature plant matter with hard or woody stems is more difficult physically for you to cut or mow and blend within the soil. It also contains higher levels of carbon, which soil microorganisms break down more slowly than nitrogen. (Flip back to Chapter 3 for an explanation of the preferred eating habits of decomposer organisms.)

When ready to harvest, chop or mow the foliage down, and then shred or break it into smaller segments for faster decomposition. If you want to plant quickly, the smaller the pieces, the less lumpy and bumpy your soil will be. If you're in no hurry to plant, larger pieces are less of a problem.

Work the organic matter into the top layer of soil, using a soil fork, shovel, or spade. (The deeper it's incorporated, the slower the decomposition rate.) Rototilling is another option for incorporating woody, coarse plant material.

Inoculating legumes

If planting a legume cover crop for the first time, coat the seeds with their appropriate rhizobial bacteria strain, called an *inoculant,* before sowing. This increases the legume's capacity to fix nitrogen. (The earlier sidebar "Fixating on nitrogen" describes the symbiotic relationship between legumes and rhizobial bacteria.) Check with your seed supplier or read catalog seed descriptions to determine which inoculant is required, because specific strains exist for different legumes. Obtain fresh inoculant and apply just before planting according to product directions.

Some legume seeds are preinoculated, so you may be able to skip the above step. For annual plantings of the same legume, it isn't necessary to reinoculate, because bacteria will remain in the soil.

If harvesting in spring, cut down cover crops when your average daily soil temperature hits 55 degrees Fahrenheit (13 degrees Celsius). This is when huge populations of soil organisms start gearing up for the decomposition process.

The following sections provide further suggestions for timing your harvest based on your goal for your soil.

Goal: Maximize the decomposition rate so nutrients are available as soon as possible for your next garden

When to harvest: Cut your crop when plants have full vegetative cover, but before blooms appear.

Fresh, moisture-rich foliage fosters a quick spike in soil microbial activity, which results in rapid decomposition of organic matter and release of nutrients. (This assumes there is also adequate moisture and aeration for decomposition to occur, as I explain in Chapter 3.)

Degree of difficulty: This is the easiest stage for you to cut and incorporate plant matter into the soil by hand.

Goal: Maximize total organic matter

When to harvest: Cut just before plants reach full bloom or when they're in full bloom.

Allow plants to develop as much organic matter (scientists call this *biomass*) as possible before producing seeds. This time frame helps promote steady decomposition of organic materials and release of nutrients into the soil over a longer period than the next option.

Degree of difficulty: Coarser plant matter is more difficult to incorporate by hand.

Goal: Maximize soil aeration and reduce compaction

When to harvest: Cut after bloom but before seeds set. Long-lasting root systems and woody, coarse plant matter enhances aeration through the soil.

Degree of difficulty: You're likely to need a rototiller or other power equipment to incorporate woody material into the soil (check out the later section "To till or not to till").

Timing is tricky if you wait to incorporate cover crops after blooming finishes. Be sure to cut plants and utilize them before they set seed. If allowed to go to seed, you may have cover crops reappearing for years to vex you! Buckwheat and hairy vetch may become invasive if allowed to go to seed.

Goal: Grow green matter to add to your compost pile

When to harvest: Cut just before plants reach full bloom or when they're in full bloom. Add foliage to your compost pile as a source of nitrogen. (See Chapter 7 for details on nitrogen ingredients.) Allow the bottoms of the plants to die in place or incorporate into the soil to add organic matter. If removing the nitrogen-rich green foliage, realize those cover crops absorbed valuable nutrients from your soil that need to be replenished with some combination of compost and fertilizer before planting your next garden.

Degree of difficulty: This is an easy stage for you to cut foliage to add to compost.

To till or not to till

Tilling (also called *rotary-tilling, rototilling,* or *rotovating*) with equipment is a labor-saving method to incorporate organic matter from your cover crops into the soil. The blades or tines of the tiller slice through the top 6 to 12 inches (15 to 30 centimeters) of soil, chopping and mixing uniformly. However, tilling also causes detrimental effects to your soil's ecosystem and structure. It kills beneficial soil organisms, such as earthworms. Overtilling pulverizes soil particles and damages soil structure, which in turn inhibits aeration and drainage and encourages compaction and erosion.

If your goal is to build soil structure bustling with microbial life (which is a major benefit of planting cover crops), you may want to limit tilling with equipment and turn the soil and incorporate organic matter by hand with a soil fork or shovel. (It's good exercise and actually kind of relaxing when you get into a rhythm.)

For larger areas where hand-turning isn't feasible, limit the overall amount of tilling. It isn't necessary to churn and pulverize everything into salt-sized bits, which ruins soil structure. Keeping the majority of the organic residue in the top few inches of soil promotes microbial activity, so try to avoid tilling too deeply. Finally, never work with or walk on wet soil, which compacts it, reducing air and water penetration.

If you prefer to be a no-till gardener, check out the next chapter for another option. It covers a soil building method that requires no digging on your part. Instead, simply spread organic matter on the soil to decompose in place.

Chapter 12

Composting in Sheets

. . . .

In This Chapter

▶ Understanding the hows and whys of sheet composting

▶ Sheet composting and planting — in tandem

. . . .

*S*heet composting is a method of enriching your soil by adding organic matter. Instead of building a compost pile or filling a bin or trench, you spread your organic matter on top of the soil in *sheets,* where it can decompose right where you need it. In this chapter I cover the advantages and disadvantages of sheet composting and explain how to do it. I conclude with an example of creating garden beds with a variant of sheet composting in which plants grow within layers of decomposing organic matter.

Sheet Composting: Read All About It

Sheet composting may remind you of other soil-improvement methods, like applying a layer of compost mulch as a top-dressing (see Chapter 9). The difference is that you want sheet compost to decompose quickly rather than remain in place to protect the soil over time. Because sheet composting provides organic matter and nutrients to the soil, it may be considered a variation of a cover crop (see Chapter 11). Unlike a cover crop, though, sheet compost doesn't have to be chopped down at the end of its life cycle — it's already dead and decomposing!

Pros and cons

Sheet composting is worth considering if you're looking for a different way to compost and enhance soil quality. This process has its advantages and disadvantages, but it's worth noting that the potential problems I outline in this section are pretty easy to avoid or fix.

Just as you decide how much time and labor to expend on any compost pile you construct, you decide how much effort to invest in sheet composting. And just like a compost pile, the more upfront effort you invest, the speedier the decomposition rate. A great advantage of sheet composting is that it's perfectly okay for busy gardeners to spread materials as they are and walk away to let them slowly decompose over time. Alternatively, you may incur a little more labor chopping organic matter into smaller pieces before spreading. You may also choose to turn your layer of sheet compost under the soil. These latter two actions speed up the decomposition process.

Although it's initially quite easy to get started, sheet composting has a few negatives that require a little extra work to overcome. Materials may be slow to decompose in comparison to a compost pile with sufficient size to create hospitable conditions for the decomposer organisms that do the bulk of the work. (Read all about these creatures and their work habits in Chapter 3.) But if you're enriching a new area and in no particular hurry, slow decomposition is an easy route to improved soil for future garden beds.

Another potential problem with sheet composting is that those hard-working decomposer organisms mentioned previously may rob the soil of all available nitrogen sources as they break down carbon mate-rials in the sheet compost layer, leaving insufficient nitrogen reserves in the soil for nearby plants to absorb. This effect is called *nitrogen immobilization.* Decomposers hold nitrogen in their bodies and recycle it repeatedly as they reproduce and die (and consume each other), until the rotting of your sheet compost is nearing completion. Then, the majority of organisms die off, releasing nitrogen stored in their bodies for plant roots to absorb. To ensure your plants don't go hungry for nitrogen, allow at least one full season up to one year for decomposition to occur before planting.

If you have thick layers of wet, nitrogen-rich materials (such as fresh grass clippings or manure), keep the process from turning anaerobic and smelly by turning these types of materials under the soil or intermixing them with layers of dry, brown materials. (Flip back to Chapter 4 for more about anaerobic composting.)

If you choose to sheet compost kitchen scraps or food waste, turn it under the soil for faster decomposition and to deter pests. After turning food scraps under, spread another layer of non-kitchen scrap materials on top of the soil, such as dried leaves or straw. Other options for composting kitchen scraps include trench composting (see Chapter 4) or using pest-proof bins (see Chapter 5).

Finally, the process of sheet composting doesn't reach sufficiently hot temperatures to kill weed seeds or plant pathogens. (For this reason, sheet composting is sometimes referred to as a "cold" method.) Be sure to eliminate any of those undesirables before spreading organic materials as sheet compost.

Where and when to lay sheets of compost

A good location for sheet composting is an area where you'd like to eventually develop a new garden. Spread layers of sheet compost and get a jump-start on soil enrichment. Other good candidates for sheet composting are existing garden beds that you don't mind letting go fallow (unplanted) for at least 3 to 12 months.

Plan on your sheet compost taking at least a full season and as much as one year to decompose before you replant. The actual time involved depends on the type of organic matter you spread, the thickness of the layer of organic matter, and how much prep work you choose to do.

When to spread sheet compost depends on your growing region and time frame for planting. If you're sheet composting to start a new bed in a year or two, timing isn't crucial, and you can simply layer materials when you have them.

If you're sheet composting atop an existing garden, apply organic matter when you've pulled spent plants at the end of your growing season. Organic materials can decompose during the dormant season when you aren't growing anything, anyway.

As long as the spent plants you pull aren't infested with pests or diseases, you can toss them on top of the soil as part of your sheet composting ingredients.

In regions with hot summers and year-round growing, sheet compost is typically spread at the end of spring gardening. Decomposition occurs over summer, and you're ready to replant when temperatures abate in fall. However, decomposition may be slow if materials dry out and summer rains are sparse. You may need to occasionally sprinkle water over your sheet compost to keep the process going.

In regions where summer is the main growing season, layer sheet compost in fall and let it decompose during winter, or winter and spring. You'll be ready to prepare soil and plant in spring or summer, depending on your local conditions and how rapidly material decomposes. Another option is apply sheet compost in summer (assuming you don't want to plant) and let it decompose until the following spring.

Getting down to ingredients

Use the same types of organic matter for sheet composting that you would add to a compost pile, including both *browns,* such as dried leaves, cardboard, and straw, and *greens,* such as grass clippings and spent garden plants. Even fresh weeds can be pulled and used as greens, as long as they don't have seeds or spread by invasive root runners that survive to infiltrate your garden. However, let other weeds wilt thoroughly first before adding them to make sure they don't survive and regrow. Refer to Chapter 7 for a list of compostable organic materials to employ with sheet composting. If you include kitchen scraps, see the warning in the "Pros and cons" section earlier in this chapter.

If you want to speed up the decomposition process for sheet composting, chop or shred organic matter into small pieces before spreading it. The smaller the initial pieces of organic matter, the more surface area is available to the decomposer organisms. Also, incorporating your sheet compost layer under the top few inches of soil after you spread it hastens decomposition. You can do this by hand with a soil fork or shovel, or use a rototiller (see caveats on tilling the soil in Chapter 11).

Use one of the following methods, depending on the ingredients you choose to incorporate in your sheet compost:

✔ Apply about 2 to 8 inches (5 to 20 centimeters) of organic material over the area to decompose in place as is. When you're ready to plant the next season, turn the remains of the organic matter under.

✔ If you have only wet, compacted materials high in nitrogen, such as fresh grass clippings or manure, apply in a thin layer (1 to 3 inches, or 2.5 to 8 centimeters). Then turn it under to speed decomposition and reduce odor potential. Alternatively, mix in wet, heavy stuff with dry, loose carbon materials, such as shredded leaves or straw.

Sheet Composting and Gardening in One Step

Spreading layers of organic matter on top of your soil as sheet compost may call to mind what you observe walking along a trail through the woods. Mother Nature piles up a wealth of organic debris — leaves, pine needles, fallen trees, animal waste, and much more. Moistened periodically by rain and snow, churned by wind, and consumed by decomposer organisms, all this debris gradually transforms into sweet-smelling humus. (Chapter 1 describes this ultimate end product of decomposition.) Amazingly diverse plant life sprouts and grows in this top layer of nutrient-rich rotted organic matter. This section explains how to copy that method in your garden.

Mimicking Mother Nature's proven methods is what permaculture is all about. Very simply stated, *permaculture* is a system of observing and copying nature to reduce humans' negative impacts on the planet. Its goal is to integrate human needs for shelter and food with a region's existing intertwined relationships among plants, animals, soils, and climate variations.

Building garden soil

Permaculture principles offer diverse techniques depending on your needs and regional characteristics. However, the following soil-building procedure (see Figure 12-1) adapted from permaculture methods works wherever you garden and provides an easy introduction to working with and benefiting from natural processes:

1. **Remove or cut any existing vegetation low to the ground, and rake the area smooth.**

2. **Sprinkle organic nitrogen fertilizer, such as alfalfa meal or cottonseed meal, to cover the area.**

   Follow recommendations on the packaging for amounts to apply.

    Blood meal and fish meal are also organic nitrogen sources. However, their scents, although not overly noticeable to humans, may attract pests, including dogs that dig with glee to find the source.

3. **Layer 6 inches (15 centimeters) of compost or aged manure on top of the nitrogen.**

   Fresh manure develops a "hot" zone as it decomposes, which may burn plant roots. If only fresh manure is available, wait at least two months to sow seeds or transplant seedlings into the mix as described in the next section.

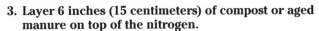

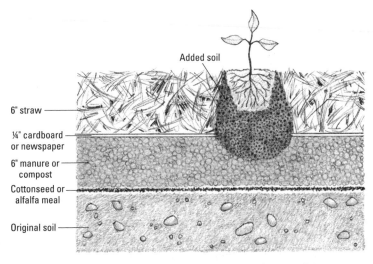

Added soil

6" straw

¼" cardboard or newspaper

6" manure or compost

Cottonseed or alfalfa meal

Original soil

Figure 12-1: Layers of sheet composting for a permaculture garden.

4. **Moisten all materials to the consistency of a wrung-out sponge.**

5. **Spread a ¼-inch-thick (6.35 millimeter) layer of cardboard and/or newspaper on top of the compost/manure layer. Weigh it down with bricks, rocks, or shovels of soil to stop it from blowing about as you work.**

6. **Soak the paper layer thoroughly with water.**

   In lieu of soaking this layer after you spread it, you can soak your paper/cardboard in a tub of water *before* spreading it.

7. **Spread 6 inches (15 centimeters) of straw as the top layer, watering it as you work to ensure even moisture throughout.**

Planting in sheet compost beds

After building your layers of organic matter as I describe in the preceding section, you're ready to plant. Take another look at Figure 12-1 and follow these steps:

1. **Pull apart the straw to create a hole the size of your fist.**

2. **Use a trowel to cut an opening in the paper/cardboard layer.**

   If the paper or cardboard is stiff, use a utility knife to cut through it. This opening allows future plant roots to spread unimpeded.

3. **Fill the hole with a handful or two of soil from an existing garden (dig some soil from the landscape if you don't yet have a garden).**

   Soil harbors zillions of local decomposer organisms ready to start breaking down organic matter in your new garden.

4. **Sow seeds or transplant seedlings into the soil.**

5. **Water and feed them as required in any garden situation.**

Planting next year's garden

Within a year's time, your organic matter layers will have broken down, and you can turn the sheet compost under to enrich the soil. Alternatively, you may also use this permaculture sheet composting method as a true "no-till" method of soil building (see Chapter 11 for details on the pluses and minuses of tilling the soil). Simply rebuild the layers as described in the earlier section "Building garden soil" to repeat the process year after year without turning the compost under.

Part V
The Part of Tens

The 5th Wave   By Rich Tennant

"Plenty of sunshine, watering, and the right compost will keep them bright and colorful. And what that won't do, a box of fluorescent felt tip markers will take care of."

In this part . . .

Grab answers fast in this part and hurry back outside to the compost pile. If you've never tried your hand at constructing a compost pile, this part's frequently asked questions give you a quick overview of the basics and calm your concerns. If you've already jumped onboard the compost train but are experiencing a bumpy ride, the troubleshooting tips will put you back on the smooth track in no time.

Chapter 13

Ten Answers to Common Questions about Compost

. . . .

. . . .

*N*ot that many years ago, most folks with even a small yard grew some of their own produce and typically had a compost pile nearby for improving their garden soil. Composting was something that people just knew how to do, and kids absorbed the skill by turning the pile or working in the garden as part of their chores! However, composting knowledge seems to have slipped by the wayside for many folks, if the number of questions I've fielded is any indication. If you're a newbie when it comes to composting, the following quick answers to commonly asked questions will get you right up to speed and ready to dig in.

What Is Compost, Really?

Compost is a blend of decayed and decaying organic materials. Although similar to compost, *humus* is organic matter that has reached its final state of decomposition. Compost may be layered on top of the soil as mulch, although other organic mulches, such as wood or bark chips, aren't sufficiently decomposed to be considered compost. You improve your garden beds by adding compost because it helps retain moisture and nutrients in sandy soil and improves drainage and aeration in clay soil. Regardless of soil type, compost improves soil structure and provides nutrients to plants. You can make compost easily from yard wastes, kitchen scraps, and household waste such as paper and cardboard.

What Are Browns and Greens?

Composters refer to organic matter that's high in carbon as *browns* and material that's high in nitrogen as *greens*. Carbon materials for composting include dry leaves, woody plant trimmings, straw, paper, cardboard, and sawdust. Grass clippings, spent garden plants, fruit and vegetable scraps, coffee grounds, tea bags, and manure are nitrogen sources. When mixing up a batch of compost, combine about three parts brown with one part green.

Can I Compost All My Kitchen Scraps? What about Pet Waste?

When it comes to compostable materials and what can and can't go in your pile or bin, it's not a free-for-all. Don't put meat, bones, fish, dairy, oils, or grease in your compost pile or bin. They may turn rancid and smelly and may attract pests, such as rodents, dogs, foxes, raccoons, and others.

Never put cat, dog, or pet bird waste in your compost. It may contain pathogens that can be transmitted to humans.

Do I Have to Purchase a Container to Compost?

Organic matter doesn't need to rot in a container. It decomposes just as well in a free-standing pile aboveground or in a hole in the ground. However, a container is a much more efficient use of space and makes it easier to produce compost faster if you maintain its contents. You can fashion a compost container from recycled materials that cost nothing, or next-to-nothing, depending on your scavenging skills. For example, four shipping pallets create a compost bin that's pretty darn close to ideal size.

Check with your area's solid waste management facility for availability of free used garbage cans repurposed as composters. Some of these agencies may also offer manufactured containers at a reduced price to encourage composting organic matter at home rather than sending it to a landfill.

Do I Have to Turn Compost Regularly?

Nope. Some pleasant day, take a break from your busy schedule and go for an amble through the woods. You won't see legions of Mother Nature's minions turning rotting organic matter with pitchforks. Yet, the forest floor is covered with lovely, black humus.

The decomposition process is ongoing all around us, whether or not we participate. As long as you're in no hurry to obtain finished compost, feel free to pile it up and let it rot on its own timetable. I recommend that laid-back gardeners follow the instructions for making basic compost in Chapter 8 to get off to a good start.

How Long before Organic Matter Becomes Compost?

"It depends" is the quick (but not terribly illuminating) answer. Factors influencing the speed of decomposition include the mix of carbon and nitrogen materials, how small the pieces are, moisture content, aeration in the pile, and the temperature of the season. In general, plan on an average of 3½ to 6 months to achieve useable compost. This time frame assumes you start with an appropriate ratio of chopped or shredded green (nitrogen) and brown (carbon) ingredients and that you moisten all the organic matter as you build a pile at least 1 cubic yard (1 cubic meter) in size. If you turn this pile two or three times to aerate and add moisture as needed, you'll harvest some compost within two months! Toss any unde-composed pieces back into the heap or into a new pile to break down further.

Obtaining compost in as little as three or four weeks is also entirely doable (see Chapter 8). Start out as I describe in the pre-ceding paragraph, and then monitor the pile's daily temperature, turning it about four times to coincide with temperature drops.

How Do I Know When My Compost Is Ready to Use?

Finished compost is dark brown — almost black — in color. Its texture is loose, crumbly, and uniform in size. Most of the original ingredients are now unrecognizable. (If there are any larger chunks of materials that haven't fully decomposed, toss them into a new pile to break down further in the next round.) If you've been main-taining a hot pile (see Chapter 3 for more on this), the composted material won't reheat after turning once it's ready to use. If you squeeze a handful of compost, it should be moist. Finished com-post smells pleasant and earthy.

Can't I Just Send My Yard and Household Waste to a Landfill to Decompose?

Why all the fuss about composting at home? It may surprise you, as it did me the first time I read about it, but organic materials don't decompose particularly well in a landfill. Heavy equipment packs and compresses the refuse so tightly that most of the air is forced out. Without oxygen, the efficient aerobic decomposer organisms (see Chapter 3) can't do their work. Garbologists, scientists who study what happens to the world's garbage, have dug down into the depths of landfills to uncover perfectly readable old newspapers and recognizable (although probably not very enticing) food items.

There are also sustainability issues related to the mountains of trash humans generate for landfills. Trucks and heavy-equipment burn gasoline and produce air pollution while hauling and burying the refuse. Many landfills have met their capacity, and there's a lack of space to build more (nobody wants a landfill in their backyard). And don't forget that methane gas, a culprit in global warming, is a byproduct of landfills.

Can I Compost in Winter?

Yes, composting can take place throughout the year. As temperatures cool, the faster-working mesophilic and thermophilic microorganisms will taper off and the cool-loving but slower-acting psychrophiles will take over. You can also insulate your pile with a thick layer of leaves, straw, or sod to help it retain heat through the winter. Some decomposition will occur, but things will really perk up again as temperatures warm in spring.

Can I Use Compost instead of Fertilizer?

Compost is considered a soil amendment or improver rather than a fertilizer. Because your compost's nutrient levels vary considerably from batch to batch due to original ingredients and method of decomposition, it's impossible to know what nutrients it contains without testing. Even so, most compost contains a wide variety of nutrients, including trace elements, to support healthy plant growth, so adding compost to your garden most certainly improves soil fertility.

Chapter 14

Ten Tips for Troubleshooting Compost

In This Chapter

▶ Determining why decomposition is slow

▶ Controlling odors and identifying critters

Composting is a fairly straightforward activity because decomposition continues whether or not you fuss over your organic matter. But if something doesn't seem quite right to you, this chapter may provide the advice you need to get your composting efforts back on track or alleviate your concerns.

Slow Decomposition

I tell you how organic matter decomposes to produce compost in Chapter 3, but like so many things in life, decomposition doesn't always go according to plan. Many factors can slow the decomposition of your compost. This list covers some of the more prominent causes and ways to combat them:

- **Lack of moisture:** A fast-decomposing compost pile contains 40 to 60 percent water. A handful of organic matter should feel damp, like a wrung-out sponge.

- **Insufficient nitrogen:** Organic matter should be about one part nitrogen (green) material to three parts carbon (brown) material. Greens are sometimes in short supply when piles get built, or they decompose so quickly that you need to add more nitrogen materials later.

- **Too much or too little mass:** The best pile size for optimal decomposition is between 3 cubic feet (3 feet tall x 3 feet wide x 3 feet deep, or 1 cubic meter) and 5 cubic feet (1.5 cubic meters). At this size, the pile can self-insulate and retain heat and moisture, but it's not so large that airflow to the center is blocked.

✔ **Poor aeration:** The aboveground efficient decomposer organisms need oxygen to thrive. As oxygen in the pile is depleted, decomposition slows. Turning the pile periodically incorporates fresh oxygen. You can also insert aeration tubes when you build a pile to improve airflow.

✔ **Cold weather:** The most productive decomposer organisms function in warm temperatures. To improve heat retention during cold weather, increase the pile size, insulate the outer edges of your pile with thick layers of straw, leaves, or sod, or cover it with a tarp.

Hovering Swarms of Teeny Flies

The bugs you may occasionally see swarming over your compost pile are the same vinegar flies you may find congregating indoors around a bowl of ripe fruit. These gnat-like flies are harmless, although you might consider them a nuisance. Gardeners in the United Kingdom call them compost flies, and in the United States, they also go by the name of fruit flies. Female vinegar flies lay eggs on fruit and vegetable skins, and the hatching larvae feed on the fungi found in rotting fruits and vegetables. To control these pesky fliers, bury kitchen scraps and food waste deep within the compost pile. When adding kitchen waste to an existing pile, cover it with an inch of soil, plus several inches of dry, brown materials, such as leaves or straw.

Fat, White Grubs

The fat, white grubs you may unearth in your pile are the larvae of various scarab beetles, such as Japanese beetles, June beetles, or dung beetles. The grubs have six legs and darker colored heads ranging from tan to reddish orange. They thrive in the moist richness of your compost pile, feeding on and breaking down rotting organic matter, which makes them beneficial indeed. If you so choose, handpick the grubs and leave them out in the open as a succulent treat for birds.

In most arid climates, these grubs aren't known to pose significant problems to living plants. However, in other climates, some species are serious pests that eat and destroy the root systems of lawns and agricultural crops. If you believe your grub population is out of control or suspect the grubs are damaging other plants, check with your county cooperative extension office or local nursery to find out which species live in your area and how to control them.

Dead Vermicomposting Worms

Worms absolutely, positively must be surrounded by moist bedding. If bedding dries out, their skin dries out, and they die. A general guideline is to maintain bedding at least 8 inches (20 centimeters) deep that has the dampness of a wrung-out sponge. Food scraps may provide additional moisture, but you can also spray extra water on your pile periodically. Worms don't want to live in a swamp, though, so be careful about excess moisture. A proper food supply also keeps your vermicomposting worms alive and squirming. Your worms will consume their bedding if no food scraps are available. For the full scoop on vermicomposting and keeping your worms alive and well, check out Chapter 10.

Lots of Bugs Crawling About

Relax, sit back, and enjoy the show! You're witnessing some of nature's decomposers at work. Bugs are a sign that all is well in your compost world. Along with billions of microorganisms you can't see without a microscope, visible macroorganisms inhabit your pile to physically break down organic matter. Common compost pile denizens include pillbugs (crawlers) and springtails (jumpers). Read more about decomposer organisms in Chapter 3.

Ammonia Odor

A properly constructed and managed compost pile does *not* smell. A strong ammonia scent is usually caused by too much nitrogen (greens). (For details on the proper balance of ingredients in your compost pile, turn to Chapter 7.) When there's an overabundance of nitrogen, the decomposer organisms can't process it fast enough, and the excess nitrogen is released to the atmosphere as ammonia. Excess moisture in the pile may also contribute to an ammonia odor. Turn the pile and add more carbon-rich materials, such as dry leaves, straw, shredded paper, or sawdust. If you purchase compost in bulk and it smells of ammonia, let it mature further before using.

Rotten Egg Odor

I repeat, a properly constructed and managed compost pile does *not* smell! If you sniff a rotten egg odor, pile contents have become compacted, compressed, and/or too wet. When air can't penetrate, aerobic decomposers fade away, and their anaerobic cousins assume control. Anaerobic decomposers give off smelly hydrogen sulfide gas as a byproduct of their efforts. That's why landfills smell bad — heavy equipment compacts the refuse and anaerobic composting organisms do all the work. In your compost pile, you're likely to have matted grass clippings, globs of fresh manure, slurry-like kitchen waste, or other high-nitrogen pockets. Introduce more oxygen by turning the entire pile, and incorporate dry leaves, straw, or shredded paper to soak up excess moisture as needed.

Slurry-Like Compost

If your compost is too thin and liquid, the cause may be your compost pile environment or its ingredients. Cover open bins or freestanding piles with a waterproof tarp. If you live in a rainy climate, consider an enclosed container (see Chapter 5). If you have a covered bin or pile and the consistency of the compost becomes too wet, spread it on the ground to dry out and/or mix it up with more dry, bulky brown materials, such as wood chips, straw, and sawdust.

Eek! A Mouse in the Compost

Mice seek warm, dry organic materials in which to build their nests. Layers of straw and leaves, especially if turned infrequently, are perfect from a mouse's perspective. To discourage mice, turn open piles regularly and moisten materials thoroughly. Rats in and around the pile are more problematic because they may spread disease to humans. Don't add potentially rat-attracting meat, bones, grease, fats, oils, or dairy products to compost piles. You can also compost in an enclosed container to keep out vermin. Read more about pest-proofing your bins in Chapter 5.

Animals Scattering Compost

Don't put meat, bones, fish, dairy, oil, or grease in your pile, which may attract animal pests. If you compost other kitchen scraps, bury them in the center of the pile. Alternatively, you can cover kitchen scraps with an inch of soil or finished compost, and then layer several more inches of dry materials on top. If the problem continues, switch to an animal-proof enclosed bin with a secure top and bottom. Chapter 5 provides recommendations on keeping animals out of compost containers without interfering with decomposition.

Index

BUSINESS, CAREERS & PERSONAL FINANCE

**Accounting For Dummies,
4th Edition***
978-0-470-24600-9

**Bookkeeping Workbook
For Dummies**†
978-0-470-16983-4

Commodities For Dummies
978-0-470-04928-0

Doing Business in China For Dummies
978-0-470-04929-7

E-Mail Marketing For Dummies
978-0-470-19087-6

**Job Interviews For Dummies,
3rd Edition***†
978-0-470-17748-8

**Personal Finance Workbook
For Dummies***†
978-0-470-09933-9

Real Estate License Exams For Dummies
978-0-7645-7623-2

Six Sigma For Dummies
978-0-7645-6798-8

**Small Business Kit For Dummies,
2nd Edition***†
978-0-7645-5984-6

Telephone Sales For Dummies
978-0-470-16836-3

BUSINESS PRODUCTIVITY & MICROSOFT OFFICE

Access 2007 For Dummies
978-0-470-03649-5

Excel 2007 For Dummies
978-0-470-03737-9

Office 2007 For Dummies
978-0-470-00923-9

Outlook 2007 For Dummies
978-0-470-03830-7

PowerPoint 2007 For Dummies
978-0-470-04059-1

Project 2007 For Dummies
978-0-470-03651-8

QuickBooks 2008 For Dummies
978-0-470-18470-7

Quicken 2008 For Dummies
978-0-470-17473-9

**Salesforce.com For Dummies,
2nd Edition**
978-0-470-04893-1

Word 2007 For Dummies
978-0-470-03658-7

EDUCATION, HISTORY, REFERENCE & TEST PREPARATION

African American History For Dummies
978-0-7645-5469-8

Algebra For Dummies
978-0-7645-5325-7

Algebra Workbook For Dummies
978-0-7645-8467-1

Art History For Dummies
978-0-470-09910-0

ASVAB For Dummies, 2nd Edition
978-0-470-10671-6

British Military History For Dummies
978-0-470-03213-8

Calculus For Dummies
978-0-7645-2498-1

**Canadian History For Dummies, 2nd
Edition**
978-0-470-83656-9

Geometry Workbook For Dummies
978-0-471-79940-5

The SAT I For Dummies, 6th Edition
978-0-7645-7193-0

Series 7 Exam For Dummies
978-0-470-09932-2

World History For Dummies
978-0-7645-5242-7

FOOD, HOME, GARDEN, HOBBIES & HOME

Bridge For Dummies, 2nd Edition
978-0-471-92426-5

**Coin Collecting For Dummies,
2nd Edition**
978-0-470-22275-1

**Cooking Basics For Dummies,
3rd Edition**
978-0-7645-7206-7

Drawing For Dummies
978-0-7645-5476-6

**Etiquette For Dummies,
2nd Edition**
978-0-470-10672-3

Gardening Basics For Dummies*†
978-0-470-03749-2

Knitting Patterns For Dummies
978-0-470-04556-5

Living Gluten-Free For Dummies†
978-0-471-77383-2

**Painting Do-It-Yourself
For Dummies**
978-0-470-17533-0

HEALTH, SELF HELP, PARENTING & PETS

Anger Management For Dummies
978-0-470-03715-7

**Anxiety & Depression Workbook
For Dummies**
978-0-7645-9793-0

Dieting For Dummies, 2nd Edition
978-0-7645-4149-0

**Dog Training For Dummies,
2nd Edition**
978-0-7645-8418-3

Horseback Riding For Dummies
978-0-470-09719-9

Infertility For Dummies†
978-0-470-11518-3

**Meditation For Dummies with CD-ROM,
2nd Edition**
978-0-471-77774-8

**Post-Traumatic Stress Disorder
For Dummies**
978-0-470-04922-8

**Puppies For Dummies,
2nd Edition**
978-0-470-03717-1

**Thyroid For Dummies,
2nd Edition**†
978-0-471-78755-6

Type 1 Diabetes For Dummies*†
978-0-470-17811-9

***** Separate Canadian edition also available
† Separate U.K. edition also available

 WILEY

INTERNET & DIGITAL MEDIA

AdWords For Dummies
978-0-470-15252-2

Blogging For Dummies, 2nd Edition
978-0-470-23017-6

Digital Photography All-in-One Desk Reference For Dummies, 3rd Edition
978-0-470-03743-0

Digital Photography For Dummies, 5th Edition
978-0-7645-9802-9

Digital SLR Cameras & Photography For Dummies, 2nd Edition
978-0-470-14927-0

eBay Business All-in-One Desk Reference For Dummies
978-0-7645-8438-1

eBay For Dummies, 5th Edition*
978-0-470-04529-9

eBay Listings That Sell For Dummies
978-0-471-78912-3

Facebook For Dummies
978-0-470-26273-3

The Internet For Dummies, 11th Edition
978-0-470-12174-0

Investing Online For Dummies, 5th Edition
978-0-7645-8456-5

iPod & iTunes For Dummies, 5th Edition
978-0-470-17474-6

MySpace For Dummies
978-0-470-09529-4

Podcasting For Dummies
978-0-471-74898-4

Search Engine Optimization For Dummies, 2nd Edition
978-0-471-97998-2

Second Life For Dummies
978-0-470-18025-9

Starting an eBay Business For Dummies, 3rd Edition†
978-0-470-14924-9

GRAPHICS, DESIGN & WEB DEVELOPMENT

Adobe Creative Suite 3 Design Premium All-in-One Desk Reference For Dummies
978-0-470-11724-8

Adobe Web Suite CS3 All-in-One Desk Reference For Dummies
978-0-470-12099-6

AutoCAD 2008 For Dummies
978-0-470-11650-0

Building a Web Site For Dummies, 3rd Edition
978-0-470-14928-7

Creating Web Pages All-in-One Desk Reference For Dummies, 3rd Edition
978-0-470-09629-1

Creating Web Pages For Dummies, 8th Edition
978-0-470-08030-6

Dreamweaver CS3 For Dummies
978-0-470-11490-2

Flash CS3 For Dummies
978-0-470-12100-9

Google SketchUp For Dummies
978-0-470-13744-4

InDesign CS3 For Dummies
978-0-470-11865-8

Photoshop CS3 All-in-One Desk Reference For Dummies
978-0-470-11195-6

Photoshop CS3 For Dummies
978-0-470-11193-2

Photoshop Elements 5 For Dummies
978-0-470-09810-3

SolidWorks For Dummies
978-0-7645-9555-4

Visio 2007 For Dummies
978-0-470-08983-5

Web Design For Dummies, 2nd Edition
978-0-471-78117-2

Web Sites Do-It-Yourself For Dummies
978-0-470-16903-2

Web Stores Do-It-Yourself For Dummies
978-0-470-17443-2

LANGUAGES, RELIGION & SPIRITUALITY

Arabic For Dummies
978-0-471-77270-5

Chinese For Dummies, Audio Set
978-0-470-12766-7

French For Dummies
978-0-7645-5193-2

German For Dummies
978-0-7645-5195-6

Hebrew For Dummies
978-0-7645-5489-6

Ingles Para Dummies
978-0-7645-5427-8

Italian For Dummies, Audio Set
978-0-470-09586-7

Italian Verbs For Dummies
978-0-471-77389-4

Japanese For Dummies
978-0-7645-5429-2

Latin For Dummies
978-0-7645-5431-5

Portuguese For Dummies
978-0-471-78738-9

Russian For Dummies
978-0-471-78001-4

Spanish Phrases For Dummies
978-0-7645-7204-3

Spanish For Dummies
978-0-7645-5194-9

Spanish For Dummies, Audio Set
978-0-470-09585-0

The Bible For Dummies
978-0-7645-5296-0

Catholicism For Dummies
978-0-7645-5391-2

The Historical Jesus For Dummies
978-0-470-16785-4

Islam For Dummies
978-0-7645-5503-9

Spirituality For Dummies, 2nd Edition
978-0-470-19142-2

NETWORKING AND PROGRAMMING

ASP.NET 3.5 For Dummies
978-0-470-19592-5

C# 2008 For Dummies
978-0-470-19109-5

Hacking For Dummies, 2nd Edition
978-0-470-05235-8

Home Networking For Dummies, 4th Edition
978-0-470-11806-1

Java For Dummies, 4th Edition
978-0-470-08716-9

Microsoft® SQL Server™ 2008 All-in-One Desk Reference For Dummies
978-0-470-17954-3

Networking All-in-One Desk Reference For Dummies, 2nd Edition
978-0-7645-9939-2

Networking For Dummies, 8th Edition
978-0-470-05620-2

SharePoint 2007 For Dummies
978-0-470-09941-4

Wireless Home Networking For Dummies, 2nd Edition
978-0-471-74940-0